Copyright © 2014 by Dr. Martin Jones

All rights reserved. This book or any portion thereof may reproduced or used in any manner whatsoever without the express written permission of the publisher except for the use of brief quotations in a book review.

ISBN-13: 978-1495244377

ISBN-10: 1495244377

http://pythonforbiologists.com

Set in PT Serif and Source Code Pro

About the author

Martin started his programming career by learning Perl during the course of his PhD in evolutionary biology, and started teaching other people to program soon after. Since then he has taught introductory programming to hundreds of biologists, from undergraduates to PIs, and has maintained a philosophy that programming courses must be friendly, approachable, and practical.

In his academic career, Martin mixed research and teaching at the University of Edinburgh, culminating in a two year stint as Lecturer in Bioinformatics. He now runs programming courses for biological researchers as a full time freelancer.

You can get in touch with Martin at

martin@pythonforbiologists.com

Martin's other works include *Python for Biologists*, *Effective Python development for Biologists* and *Python for complete beginners*.

Table of Contents

1: Introduction — 1

About this book » 1
Why use Python's advanced features? » 1
How to use this book » 2
Exercises and solutions » 5
A note on setting up your environment » 6
Joined-up programming » 7
Getting in touch » 8

2: Recursion and trees — 9

Recursively generating kmers » 9
Processing tree-like data » 16
Recap » 28
Exercise » 30
Solution » 31

3: Complex data structures — 36

Tuples » 36
Sets » 38
Lists of lists » 40
Lists of dicts and lists of tuples » 42
Other complex structures » 45
Recap » 55
Exercises » 57
Solutions » 58

4: Object-oriented Python — 64

Introduction » 64
A simple DNA sequence class » 66
Constructors » 70
Inheritance » 76
Overriding » 85
Calling methods in the superclass » 87

Polymorphism » 89
Recap » 90
Exercise » 92
Solution » 93

5: Functional Python   109

Introduction » 109
State and mutability » 109
Side effects » 110
Functions as objects » 113
What is to be calculated » 116
Built-in higher order functions » 117
map » 117
filter » 122
sorted » 124
reduce » 129
Writing higher-order functions » 131
Recap » 137
Exercises » 138
Solutions » 141

6: Iterators, comprehensions & generators   157

Defining lists » 157
Lists and iterables » 158
List comprehensions » 159
Dictionary comprehensions » 163
Set comprehensions » 165
Iterators and generators » 165
Recap » 171
Exercises » 172
Solutions » 173

7: Exception handling   180

Catching exceptions » 181
Catching specific errors » 183
else blocks in exception handling » 188
finally blocks in exception handling » 189

Nested try/except blocks » 193
Exceptions bubble up » 194
Raising exceptions » 197
Custom exception types » 200
Recap » 202
Exercises » 204
Solutions » 208

1: Introduction

About this book

Welcome to *Advanced Python for Biologists*. As I was completing my first book *Python for Biologists* I realized that, although it covered all the core parts of the language, I had to leave out some of the most elegant and useful parts of Python, so I was already thinking about the sequel. The purpose of this book is to continue the exploration of the Python language where the previous book left off, with the goal that between them, the two books will cover every useful part of the Python language. The overarching philosophy of this book is exactly the same as the previous one: to illustrate Python features using relevant biological examples which will be useful in real life. Just as before, the emphasis is on Python as a tool for practical problem-solving.

Why use Python's advanced features?

If you've read and understood *Python for Biologists*, or indeed any introductory Python programming book, then you probably have all the programming tools that you need to solve any given problem. Why, then, is it necessary to have an entire second book devoted to advanced features of Python? One reason is that in order to understand code that you find in the wild, you need to have a thorough overview of the language. You may be able to get on perfectly well in your own programming career without ever writing a class, a lambda expression, or a list comprehension, but when you come across these techniques in other people's code (and you will), you'll need to know how they work.

A second, more persuasive reason is that all the features of Python that we are going to discuss in this book have been added to the language for good reasons – because they make code easier to write, easier to maintain, easier to test, faster, or more efficient. You don't *have* to use objects when modelling biological systems – but it will make development much easier. You don't *have* to use comprehensions when transforming data – but doing so will allow you to express your ideas much more concisely. You don't *have* to use recursive functions when processing tree-like data – but your code will be much more readable if you do.

Yet another reason is that knowing about features of Python opens up new approaches to programming, which will allow you to think about problems in a new light. For example, two large chapters in this book are devoted to object oriented programming and functional programming. The aim of these chapters is to introduce you not only to object oriented and functional features, but also to object oriented and functional approaches to tackling real life problems.

Hopefully, as you encounter new tools and techniques in this book the biological examples will convince you that they're useful things to know about. I have tried, for each new concept introduced, to point out why and in what circumstances it is a better way of doing things than the way that you might already know.

How to use this book

Picking the order of chapters in Python for Biologists was a straightforward affair, because the concepts and tools followed a natural progression. Picking the order of chapters for this book has been much trickier, because the features and techniques we are going to look at tend to be used together. In other words, whichever way I arrange the chapters, there are inevitably some cases where material from one chapter relies on material from a later chapter. I've tried to minimize such cases, and have added footnotes to point out connections between chapters whenever possible. If there's a particular chapter that sounds interesting then it's fine to jump in and start reading there; just be aware that you'll probably have to skip around in the book a bit to fill in any gaps in your current knowledge.

Chapters tend to follow a predictable structure. They generally start with a few paragraphs outlining the motivation behind the features that it will cover – why do they exist, what problems do they allow us to solve, and why are they useful in biology specifically? These are followed by the main body of the chapter in which we discuss the relevant features and how to use them. The length of the chapters varies quite a lot – sometimes we want to cover a topic briefly, other times we need more depth. This section ends with a brief recap outlining what we have learned, followed by exercises and solutions (more on that topic below).

The book assumes that you're familiar with all the material in *Python for Biologists*. If you have some Python experience, but haven't read *Python for Biologists*, then it's probably worth downloading a free copy and at least looking over the chapter contents to make sure you're comfortable with them. I will sometimes refer in the text or in footnotes to sections of *Python for Biologists* – rather than repeating the URL where you can get a copy[1], I'll simply give it here:

```
http://pythonforbiologists.com
```

---

1 If you're reading this book as an ebook (as opposed to a physical book) then you should have received a copy of *Python for Biologists* in your download.

Formatting

A book like this has lots of special types of text – we'll need to look at examples of Python code and output, the contents of files, and technical terms. Take a minute to note the typographic conventions we'll be using.

In the main text of this book, **bold type** is used to emphasize important points and *italics* for technical terms and filenames. Where code is mixed in with normal text it's written in a `monospaced font like this` with a grey background. Occasionally there are footnotes[1] to provide additional information that is interesting to know but not crucial to understanding, or to give links to web pages.

Example Python code is highlighted with a solid border and the name of the matching example file is written just underneath the example to the right:

```
Some example code goes here
```
example.py

Not every bit of code has a matching example file – much of the time we'll be building up a Python program bit by bit, in which case there will be a single example file containing the finished version of the program. The example files are in separate folders, one for each chapter, to make them easy to find.

Sometimes it's useful to refer to a specific line of code inside an example. For this, we'll use numbered circles like this❶:

```
a line of example code
another line of example code
this is the important line❶
here is another line
```

---

1   Like this.

Chapter 1: Introduction

Example output (i.e. what we see on the screen when we run the code) is highlighted with a dotted border:

```
Some output goes here
```

Often we want to look at the code and the output it produces together. In these situations, you'll see a solid-bordered code block followed immediately by a dotted-bordered output block.

Other blocks of text (usually file contents or typed command lines) don't have any kind of border and look like this:

```
contents of a file
```

Often when looking at larger examples, or when looking at large amounts of output, we don't need to see the whole thing. In these cases, I'll use ellipses (...) to indicate that some text has been missed out.

I have used UK English spelling throughout, which I hope will not prove distracting to US readers.

In programming, we use different types of brackets for different purposes, so it's important to have different names for them. Throughout this book, I will use the word *parentheses* to refer to (), *square brackets* to refer to [], and *curly brackets* to refer to {}.

Exercises and solutions

Each chapter is accompanied by one or more exercises and solutions. You can always download the most recent version of the exercise files and solutions from this address:

```
http://pythonforbiologists.com/index.php/exercise-files/
```

The number and complexity of exercises differ greatly between chapters depending on the nature of the material. Compared to the exercises in *Python for Biologists*, the exercises in this book are fewer in number but more complicated. Many of the exercise problems are written in a deliberately vague manner and the exact details of how the solutions work is up to you (very much like real life programming!) You can always look at the solutions to see one possible way of tackling the problem, but there are often multiple valid approaches.

I **strongly** recommend that you try tackling the exercises yourself before reading the solutions; there really is no substitute for practical experience when learning to program. I also encourage you to adopt an attitude of curious experimentation when working on the exercises – if you find yourself wondering if a particular variation on a problem is solvable, or if you recognize a closely-related problem from your own work, try solving it! Continuous experimentation is a key part of developing as a programmer, and the quickest way to find out what a particular function or feature will do is to try it.

The example solutions to exercises are written in a different way to most programming textbooks: rather than simply present the finished solution, I have outlined the thought processes involved in solving the exercises and shown how the solution is built up step-by-step. Hopefully this approach will give you an insight into the problem-solving mindset that programming requires. It's probably a good idea to read through the solutions even if you successfully solve the exercise problems yourself, as they sometimes suggest an approach that is not immediately obvious.

A note on setting up your environment

This book assumes that you have a working Python 2 or Python 3 environment to work in, and that you're comfortable running programs

Chapter 1: Introduction

on the command line and editing them in a text editor. For notes on setting up your environment, see the introductory chapter in *Python for Biologists*. I've tried to ensure that all code samples and exercise solutions will work in both Python 2 and Python 3 – where there are differences between versions, I have noted it in the text.

There are two chief differences that are relevant to multiple examples and exercises. Firstly, to carry out floating point division in Python 2 we need to include the line

```
from __future__ import division
```

at the start of our programs. Secondly, the way that we get input from the user is slightly different: in Python 3 we use the `input` function and in Python 2 we use the `raw_input` function.

Joined-up programming

Finally, a quick note about synergy between chapters. When explaining new concepts, I've made the examples as simple as possible in the interests of clarity and avoided using multiple "advanced" techniques in a single example. For instance, in the chapter on object oriented programming I've given examples of class methods that don't use any of the techniques from other chapters.

This makes it easier for the reader to concentrate on the new material while being able to easily understand the context. But it can lead to the misconception that these programming techniques are mutually exclusive. In fact, nothing could be further from the truth: the real power of the tools that we're going to be discussing comes when they are used together. So it's certainly possible, for example, to write a class (chapter 4) that stores some data in a list of dicts (chapter 3) and has methods that use recursion (chapter 2) and raise custom exceptions (chapter 7). You just won't see such code in the examples, because it wouldn't be a very good way of introducing the new material!

What's not covered

There are several topics that you might expect to find in an advanced programming book that are not here. In this book, I've focussed purely on aspects of the core Python language, and avoided talking about subjects that are more related to the development process. If you want to read about:

- Python's packaging and distribution system
- performance and speeding up code
- about automated testing
- building user interfaces
- logging

Then take a look at *Effective Python development for Biologists* by the same author. Where sections from that book are particularly relevant to sections here, I've tried to mention them in footnotes.

Getting in touch

Learning to program is a difficult task, and my one goal in writing this book is to make it as easy and accessible as possible to get started. So, if you find anything that is hard to understand, or you think may contain an error, please get in touch – just drop me an email at

martin@pythonforbiologists.com

Chapter 1: Introduction

and I promise to get back to you. If you find the book useful, then please also consider leaving an Amazon review to help other people find it.

2: Recursion and trees

A concise definition of recursion, when we're talking about programming languages, is this: *writing code which calls itself.* If you've never encountered recursion before, this definition isn't very helpful, since it fails to answer two key questions: why is recursion useful, and how do we do it in Python?

The second question is straightforward to answer: Python has a very simple syntax for recursion that we'll see in the examples in this chapter.

The first question is trickier to answer. Recursion is useful because it allows us to write code which solves problems which have a *tree-like* structure. Much of the rest of this chapter is devoted to illustrating examples of biological problems that fall into this category, which turns out to include more types of problems than we might initially think.

We'll start with a problem that, at first, appears to have nothing to do with trees.....

Recursively generating kmers

Many bioinformatics problems involve working with *kmers*: short DNA sequences of a given length (we usually refer to the length using the letter k, hence the name). One obvious questions concerning kmers is this: given a length k, how can we generate a list of all the possible kmers of that length? If we pick a small value for k – for example, three – then we can write a series of nested `for` loops to generate all possible sequences:

Chapter 2: Recursion and trees

```
def generate_trimers():
    bases = ['A', 'T', 'G', 'C']
    result = []
    for base1 in bases:
        for base2 in bases:
            for base3 in bases:
                result.append(base1 + base2 + base3)
    return result
```

generate_3mers.py

In the above example, we have three nested `for` loops which iterate over the same list of four possible bases. The outer `for` loop defines the first base of the 3mer, the middle `for` loop defines the second base, and the inner `for` loop defines the third base. Because each `for` loop repeats four times (one for each base) the `append()` line gets called 4x4x4 = 64 times, so we end up with a list of all possible 3mers.

Suppose we wanted to modify this code to generate 4mers instead of 3mers. We would simply add another `for` loop inside the original three. But what if we wanted to write a function that would do the same job, but for **any** value of k – in other words, for sequences of any length? This is a very tricky problem. We know that we need to use a `for` loop to add bases onto the end of a growing sequence, but the difficult part is making sure that we keep all the possible sequences between iterations. Here's one possible solution:

```
def generate_kmers(length):
    result = [''] ❶
    for i in range(length): ❷
        new_result = [] ❹
        for kmer in result:
            for base in ['A', 'T', 'G', 'C']:
                new_result.append(kmer + base) ❸
        result = new_result ❺
    return result
```

generate_kmers.py

The function works in the following way: we start off with a list containing a single empty string – this is the starting point for each of our final sequences❶ . Then, we extend each element in that list (initially just one element, but as we'll see, the size of the list will grow) in an iterative process (controlled using a `for` loop and a `range`❷). To extend a sequence, we add each of the four possible bases onto the end❸. Because we want to end up with the final sequences (i.e. we don't want the intermediate steps) we have to create a new temporary list❹ to hold the extended sequences for each round of extension, and then use that list as the list of sequences for the next round❺. After each iteration of the `for` loop, two thing happen: the results list contains four times as many elements as before (because we've added each of the four possible bases) and those elements are one base longer than before.

Why does this function look so different to the `generate_trimers()` function? In the `generate_trimers()` function we use nested loops to generate the sequences, because we know in advance how long we want the sequences to be – three bases means that we need three nested loops. But in the function above, we can't use nested loops, because we don't know in advance how many loops we'll need. The number of loops depends on the length of the kmers. **What we require is a way to express the idea of nesting code an arbitrary number of times**.

Recursion is the way to express this, but to understand it, we need to think about the problem in a slightly different way. Here's an English translation of the `generate_kmers()` function above:

> *"Start with a list containing a single empty string. Next, extend each element in the list by adding each of the four possible bases onto the end. Repeat this extension process as many times as necessary until the sequences are the length you require"*

Chapter 2: Recursion and trees

That explanation is what we might call an *imperative description* of how to generate all possible kmers of a given length. It gives step-by-step instructions which we can follow to get the result we want. But there's another solution to the problem, which we can describe in a totally different way:

> *"To get a list of all kmers of a given length, start by checking the length. If the length is one then the result is simply a list of the four bases. If the length is more than one, take the list of all possible sequences whose length is one less that the length you're looking for, and add each of the four possible bases to each of its elements to get the result."*

At first glance, this doesn't seem like a very helpful solution. Rather than telling us **how to figure out** the answer, it just describes **what the answer looks like**. And it assumes that we have a way to magically calculate the list of all possible sequences that are one base shorter than the length we want. But – remarkably – when we write a function using this description, it actually works:

```
def generate_kmers_rec(length):
    if length == 1:                                    ❶
        return ['A', 'T', 'G', 'C']                    ❷
    else:
        result = []
        for seq in generate_kmers_rec(length - 1):     ❸
            for base in ['A', 'T', 'G', 'C']:          ❹
                result.append(seq + base)
        return result
```

generate_kmers_recursive.py

To understand what's going on, here's the written description again showing which line of code corresponds to each bit:

"If the length is one❶ then the result is simply a list of the four bases❷. To get the result when the length is more than one, take the list of all possible sequences whose length is one less that the length you're looking for❸, and add each of the four possible bases to it❹."

The magic occurs where the `generate_kmers_rec()` function **calls itself❺**. This is what we mean by a recursive function – one that calls itself (with different parameters) in order to generate its result. This is unintuitive, to say the least, the first time you encounter it!

Let's follow what happens step by step when we call the function with a length of three – i.e. when we evaluate `generate_kmers_rec(3)`. The first thing that happens is that the function checks whether the `length` is equal to one. This turns out to be false (because the `length` is 3), so the `else` block is executed. A new empty list called `result` is created, and then the function calls `generate_kmers_rec(2)` in order to get the list of kmers of length 2. Inside the call to `generate_kmers_rec(2)`, the first few steps repeat. We test whether the `length` variable is equal to one and when the answer is no, we enter the `else` block and create a new empty list called `result`.

Note that at this point, we have two empty lists called `result` – one belonging to the `generate_kmers_rec(3)` call, and one belonging to the `generate_kmers_rec(2)` call. There is nothing out-of-the-ordinary about this – we use multiple functions with the same variable names all the time in our code, and it works because of Python's scoping rules.

Next, we need to figure out the list of all sequences of length one, so we make a call to `generate_kmers_rec(1)`. At the start of this function call, we examine the `length` variable and find that it is equal to one, so the function immediately returns the list `['A', 'T', 'G', 'C']` and the function call is over. Now the call to `generate_kmers_rec(2)` can carry on running. It takes that list, adds each of the four bases to each of the four sequences to generate a list of the 16 dinucleotides, and returns that list. The list of dinucleotides is received by `generate_kmers_rec(3)`, which finishes the job by adding each of the four bases to each of the 16 dinucleotides to create a list of 64 trinucletoides, and returning it.

When looking at a recursive function like the one above, an obvious question is: *why doesn't the function run forever?* If every time the function is called, it calls itself again, then why don't we end up with an infinite number of function calls which never return[1]? In our example above, the answer lies in the special case where the length is one. We can see by looking at the function definition that each call to the function will trigger another call to the function **unless** the length is one. Couple that fact with the fact that we decrease the length by one whenever the function calls itself, and we can see that whatever length is supplied as the argument to the initial function call, eventually the function will be called with a length of one, at which point the functions will start to return.

In general, these two criteria are necessary for any recursive function to work properly: there **must** be a special case that causes the function to return without calling itself, and there **must** be some guarantee that this special case will eventually be reached.

In the introduction to this chapter, we said that recursion is good for solving problems that have a *tree-like structure*. The problem of generating all kmers of a given length is an example, although the tree-

---

[1] It is actually quite easy to write functions that never return when getting started with recursive programming!

Chapter 2: Recursion and trees

like nature of the problem isn't obvious. To make it clearer, imagine the process of choosing a single 3mer by selecting one base at a time. At the start of the process, we have four options – four different **branches** – one for each base:

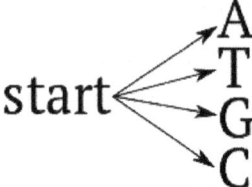

We choose one of these paths – for instance, the one labelled T – and then are faced with four more branches:

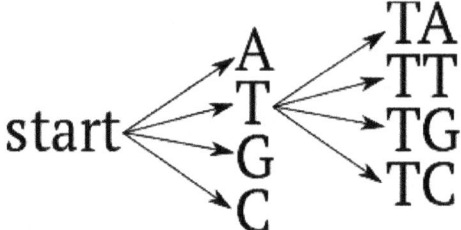

This time we pick the branch labelled TG. Finally, we have a choice of four different branches to end up at one of four different 3mers:

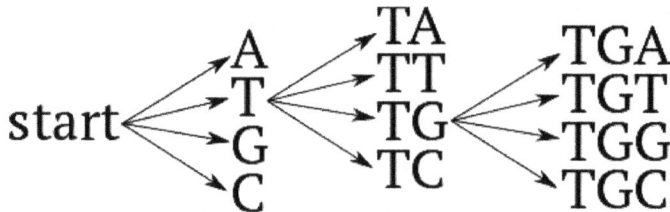

Chapter 2: Recursion and trees

Viewed like this, it's clear why we can consider this a tree-like problem: generating all possible kmers of a given length is equivalent to visiting all the leaves of the tree.

In the above example, there's not a clear winner between the *iterative* solution and the *recursive* solution – both are roughly equally easy to read. In the next section, we'll consider some data that are more explicitly tree-like and see some examples of problems where recursion is clearly the best solution.

Processing tree-like data

Child-to-parent trees

Suppose we want to store some information about taxonomic relationships among primates. If we were describing the taxonomy of primates using natural language, here are two statements that we might make: "*Homo sapiens is a member of the group Homo, which is a member of the group Homininae*" and "*Primates contains two groups – Haplorrhini and Strepsirrhini*".

These two statements are similar – they are both talking about group membership – but they approach the problem of description in different ways. The first expresses the relationship in *child to parent* terms, and the second in *parent to child*. How might we store these relationships in a Python program? The first can be stored quite simply: we can create a dictionary which holds child → parent relationships:

```
tax_dict = {
    'Homo sapiens' : 'Homo',
    'Homo' : 'Homininae'
}
```

In the above code we have a dictionary with two elements, each one describing a single child-to-parent relationship.

Storing parent-to-child relationships looks a bit different. To store the second set of relationships we can create a list and store it in a variable:

```
primates_children = ['Haplorrhini', 'Strepsirrhini']
```

Note that this looks a little less satisfying – the name of the parent (Primates) is a variable name, while the names of the child taxa are strings.

The outlook for parent-to-child relationships looks even worse when we start to consider how we would store additional relationships. To add the relationships from the first statement requires us to create two new variables:

```
primates_children = ['Haplorrhini', 'Strepsirrhini']
homo_children = ['Homo sapiens']
homininae_children = ['homo']
```

As before, we have an odd mixture of variable names and strings, and one-element lists for any parent that has only a single child. We can quickly see that adding more relationships under the parent-to-child scheme is going to result in some very unwieldy code!

By contrast, we can store all the relationships using the child-to-parent scheme by simply adding extra items to the dict:

```
tax_dict = {
    'Homo sapiens' : 'Homo',
    'Homo' : 'Homininae',
    'Haplorrhini' : 'Primates',
    'Strepsirrhini' : 'Primates'
}
```

Chapter 2: Recursion and trees

Let's consider a bigger example. Here's a taxonomy showing a selection of primate taxa. Hopefully the meaning of the layout is obvious: child taxa are indented underneath their parent:

```
Primates
   Haplorrhini
      Simiiformes
         Hominoidea
            Pan troglodytes
            Pongo abelii
      Tarsiiformes
         Tarsius tarsier
   Strepsirrhini
      Lorisidae
         Loris tardigradus
      Lemuriformes
         Allocebus trichotis
      Lorisiformes
         Galago alleni
         Galago moholi
```

Here's the corresponding dict, storing the relationships as key/value pairs just as before:

```
tax_dict = {
'Pan troglodytes' : 'Hominoidea',      'Pongo abelii' : 'Hominoidea',
'Hominoidea' : 'Simiiformes',          'Simiiformes' : 'Haplorrhini',
'Tarsius tarsier' : 'Tarsiiformes',    'Haplorrhini' : 'Primates',
'Tarsiiformes' : 'Haplorrhini',        'Loris tardigradus' : 'Lorisidae',
'Lorisidae' : 'Strepsirrhini',         'Strepsirrhini' : 'Primates',
'Allocebus trichotis' : 'Lemuriformes', 'Lemuriformes' : 'Strepsirrhini',
'Galago alleni' : 'Lorisiformes',      'Lorisiformes' : 'Strepsirrhini',
'Galago moholi' : ' Lorisiformes'
}
```

Even with some white space added to make the items in the dict line up, it's not particularly easy to read! Nevertheless, every relationship in the tree is also present in the dict, so we can be confident that it represents the whole taxonomy.

What can we do with this data structure once it's been created? Let's try writing a function that will list all the parents[1] of a given taxon. When given the name of a taxon as input, it will return a list of all the taxa of which that taxon is a member. For example, given the input `'Galago alleni'` it should return the list `['Lorisiformes', 'Strepsirrhini', 'Primates']`. If we know the number of ancestors of the node in advance, we can write a function that will do the job in a slightly clunky way:

```
def get_ancestors(taxon):
    first_parent = tax_dict.get(taxon)
    second_parent = tax_dict.get(first_parent)
    third_parent = tax_dict.get(second_parent)
    return[first_parent, second_parent, third_parent]
```

get_three_parents.py

We use the dictionary to look up the parent for the node, then use it again to look up the parent of the parent, etc. etc. Obviously this will fail when we try to use it on a node that doesn't have exactly three ancestors.

Here's an alternative way to write the function that doesn't rely on us knowing the number of ancestors in advance. We'll use a `while` loop to keep going up the tree until we reach Primates:

---

1   In the tree sense, not the biological sense!

Chapter 2: Recursion and trees

```
def get_ancestors(taxon):
    result = [taxon]
    while taxon != 'Primates':
        result.append(tax_dict.get(taxon))
        taxon = tax_dict.get(taxon) ❶
    return result
```

get_parents_while.py

Notice how each time round the loop❶ we set the value of the taxon variable to be the name of the parent taxon, which then becomes the child in the next iteration of the `while` loop[1].

Here's another function that does the same job using recursion:

```
def get_ancestors(taxon):
    if taxon == 'Primates':    ❶
        return [taxon]          ❷
    else:
        parent = tax_dict.get(taxon)   ❸
        parent_ancestors = get_ancestors(parent)
        return [parent] + parent_ancestors  ❹
```

get_parents_recursive.py

This uses a totally different approach to the previous examples. In this version of the function, we consider two different cases for the input taxon❶ . If the input taxon is 'Primates', then we know that it doesn't have any ancestors (i.e. it is at the top of the tree) so return a list containing just the taxon itself❷. If the taxon isn't 'Primates', then we know that the list of its ancestors is its parent, plus the ancestors of its parent. In this case we look up the parent❸ and then calculate the parent's ancestors – this is the recursive call. Finally we return the answer we are looking for – a list made up of the parent, and the parent's ancestors❹.

---

[1] This is very similar to the way that the long sequences of a given iteration become the short sequences of the next iteration in our kmer example at the start of the chapter.

Chapter 2: Recursion and trees

Just as in our kmers example, the recursive function works because there is a special case for which the function doesn't call itself (the case where the input taxon is 'Primates'). Let's see how this function works in detail by adding a few `print()` statements and calling it:

```
def get_ancestors(taxon):
    print('calculating ancestors for ' + taxon)
    if taxon == 'Primates':
        print('taxon is Primates, returning an empty list')
        return []
    else:
        print('taxon is not Primates, looking up the parent')
        parent = tax_dict.get(taxon)
        print('the parent is ' + parent + ' ')
        print('looking up ancestors for ' + parent)
        parent_ancestors = get_ancestors(parent)
        print('parent ancestors are ' + str(parent_ancestors))
        result = [parent] + parent_ancestors
        print('about to return the result: ' + str(result))
        return result

get_ancestors('Galago alleni')
```

get_parents_verbose.py

This looks like a lot of extra code, but all we have done is added a temporary result variable to hold the result, and added a lot of `print()` statements. If we look at the output from this code we can see exactly what is going on:

Chapter 2: Recursion and trees

```
calculating ancestors for Galago alleni ❶
taxon is not Primates, looking up the parent
the parent is Lorisiformes ❷
looking up ancestors for Lorisiformes
calculating ancestors for Lorisiformes
taxon is not Primates, looking up the parent
the parent is Strepsirrhini
looking up ancestors for Strepsirrhini
calculating ancestors for Strepsirrhini
taxon is not Primates, looking up the parent
the parent is Primates
looking up ancestors for Primates ❸
calculating ancestors for Primates
taxon is Primates, returning an empty list
parent ancestors are []
about to return the result: ['Primates']
parent ancestors are ['Primates']
about to return the result: ['Strepsirrhini', 'Primates']
parent ancestors are ['Strepsirrhini', 'Primates']
about to return the result: ['Lorisiformes', 'Strepsirrhini', 'Primates']
['Lorisiformes', 'Strepsirrhini', 'Primates']
```

We start the function with the input `'Galago alleni'`❶. We check if it's equal to `'Primates'`, and find that it's not so we look up the parent❷ and find out that it's `'Lorisiformes'`. The next step in the code is to look up the ancestors for the parent, so we start the `get_ancestors()` function again, but this time with `'Lorisiformes'` as the input taxon. We continue in this way until we finally try to calculate the ancestors for `'Primates'`❸. This time, rather than starting off a new call to `get_ancestors()`, we return an empty string. This allows the call to `get_ancestors('Lorisiformes')` to return, which allows the previous call to `get_ancestors()` to return, and so on all the way back to the initial call. You can see from the output how all the "about to return the result" `print()` statements pile up near the end.

A handy way to visualize what's going on in recursive functions is to add spaces to the start of each `print()` statement to represent how many times the function has been called[1]. Here's a variation of our function that does just that. We have to add an extra argument to store the depth of the function call, which we increase by one each time we call the function (except for the initial call, where we supply a depth of 0):

```
def get_ancestors(taxon, depth):
    spacer = ' ' * depth
    print(spacer + 'calculating ancestors for ' + taxon)
    if taxon == 'Primates':
        print(spacer + 'taxon is Primates, returning an empty list')
        return []
    else:
        print(spacer + 'taxon is not Primates, looking up the parent')
        parent = tax_dict.get(taxon)
        print(spacer + 'the parent is ' + parent + ' ')
        print(spacer + 'looking up ancestors for ' + parent)
        parent_ancestors = get_ancestors(parent, depth + 1)
        print(spacer + 'parent ancestors are ' + str(parent_ancestors))
        result = [parent] + parent_ancestors
        print(spacer + 'about to return the result: ' + str(result))
        return result

get_ancestors('Galago alleni', 0)
```

get_parents_indented.py

In this version of the function, at the start of each function call we create a variable called `spacer` which is just a string of space characters, then print the spacer at the start of each line of output. Now the output clearly shows how the levels of function calls build up, then collapse:

---

1 The technical term for this is the *depth* of the *call stack.*

Chapter 2: Recursion and trees

```
calculating ancestors for Galago alleni
taxon is not Primates, looking up the parent
the parent is Lorisiformes
looking up ancestors for Lorisiformes
  calculating ancestors for Lorisiformes
  taxon is not Primates, looking up the parent
  the parent is Strepsirrhini
  looking up ancestors for Strepsirrhini
    calculating ancestors for Strepsirrhini
    taxon is not Primates, looking up the parent
    the parent is Primates
    looking up ancestors for Primates
      calculating ancestors for Primates
      taxon is Primates, returning an empty list
    parent ancestors are []
    about to return the result: ['Primates']
  parent ancestors are ['Primates']
  about to return the result: ['Strepsirrhini', 'Primates']
parent ancestors are ['Strepsirrhini', 'Primates']
about to return the result: ['Lorisiformes', 'Strepsirrhini',
'Primates']
```

Parent-to-child trees

In the previous section, we started off by comparing two different ways of storing tree-like data, and concluded that storing child-to-parent relationships was easier than storing parent-to-child relationships. That's certainly the case for the example code that we looked at, but here I want to introduce an approach that makes parent-to-child relationships look a lot better.

Let's start with a simple question: why, in the examples in the previous section, could we use a dictionary to store child → parent relationships, but not parent → child relationships? Answer: because keys in a dictionary have to be unique, so we can't store multiple key value pairs for parents that have more than one child. In other words, we can't store the three children of Strepsirrhini like this:

```
tax_dict = {
    'Strepsirrhini' : 'Lorisidae',
    'Strepsirrhini' : 'Lemuriformes',
    'Strepsirrhini' : 'Lorisiformes'
}
```

because the third item would overwrite the previous two.

What we can do, however, is create a single item where the key is the name of the parent taxon, and the value is a **list** of the names of the child taxa[1]:

```
tax_dict = {
    'Strepsirrhini' : ['Lorisidae', 'Lemuriformes','Lorisiformes']
}
```

Using this approach, we can store the exact same set of relationships as before in a parent → child manner:

```
new_tax_dict = {
    'Primates': ['Haplorrhini', 'Strepsirrhini'],
    'Tarsiiformes': ['Tarsius tarsier'],
    'Haplorrhini': ['Tarsiiformes', 'Simiiformes'],
    'Simiiformes': ['Hominoidea'],
    'Lorisidae': ['Loris tardigradus'],
    'Lemuriformes': ['Allocebus trichotis'],
    'Lorisiformes': ['Galago alleni','Galago moholi'],
    'Hominoidea': ['Pongo abelii', 'Pan troglodytes'],
    'Strepsirrhini': ['Lorisidae', 'Lemuriformes', 'Lorisiformes']
}
```

Now we can start to address a problem that is a mirror of the one in the previous section: given a taxon, how do we find all its **children**? Just like before, we'll look at both iterative and recursive solutions. Here's an

---

[1] This idea – of storing a list in a dict – is explored in much more depth in the chapter on complex data structures.

Chapter 2: Recursion and trees

iterative function that returns a list of all the children of the taxon which is given as its argument:

```
def get_children(taxon):
    result = []
    stack = [taxon] ❶
    while len(stack) != 0:
        current_taxon = stack.pop() ❷
        current_taxon_children = new_tax_dict.get(current_taxon, [])
        stack.extend(current_taxon_children) ❸
        result.append(current_taxon) ❹

    return result
```

get_children.py

It's not the easiest function to read, so here's a line-by-line explanation. We start off by creating a list to hold the result and a list called `stack`[1] which will hold the names of the taxa that we need to consider❶. Initially, the stack holds just one element – the taxon that was given as the argument. We then enter a `while` loop which keeps executing as long as the length of the stack is positive – i.e. as long as the stack still holds some taxa to be processed. To process a taxon from the stack, we first remove it using `pop()`❷, then look up its children in the dictionary. We add any children that we find onto the end of the stack❸ and then add the taxon itself to the result❹.

Here's some code that calls the function on a couple of different input taxa:

```
print(get_children('Strepsirrhini'))
print(get_children('Lorisiformes'))
```

And here's the output. The result of the first call is wrapped over two lines as it's too long to fit on the page, but it's still just a single list. Notice that

---

1 A *stack* is the traditional computer science name for a list where elements are added and removed from the top – picture a stack of dinner plates.

the input taxon is included in the list – we could modify the function to remove it, but it's not important for the purposes of this discussion:

```
['Strepsirrhini', 'Lorisiformes', 'Galago moholi', 'Galago
alleni', 'Lemuriformes', 'Allocebus trichotis', 'Lorisidae',
'Loris tardigradus']
['Lorisiformes', 'Galago moholi', 'Galago alleni']
```

The best way to understand how the function works is to picture the fate of a single taxon as we encounter it. Each taxon is first added onto the `stack` variable at the point where we are processing its parent. It is then (at some point in the future) transferred from the `stack` variable to the result variable, having its own children added to the `stack` variable in the process. In this manner, taxa are repeatedly added onto and removed from the stack, until the stack is empty, the `while` loop ends and the function can return.

Contrast the code above with the recursive function:

```
def get_children_rec(taxon):
    result = [taxon]  ❶
    children = new_tax_dict.get(taxon, [])  ❷
    for child in children:
        result.extend(get_children_rec(child))  ❸
    return result
```

get_children_recursive.py

Here, we create a single result list❶, which at the start of the function contains just the taxon that was given as the argument. The, we look up the children of that taxon❷ , and for each child, we add its children to the result using a recursive function call❸. Then we simply return the list. Or in other words:

> *"The list of all children of a taxon is the taxon itself plus, for each child, a list of their children"*

Chapter 2: Recursion and trees

Why is the recursive solution so much simpler and clearer than the iterate solution for this case? One way to look at it to consider the nature of a tree-like data structure such as the one we're using to store the taxonomy. We can describe a taxonomic tree is like this: *a node in a tree has a name and some children. The children of a node are also nodes themselves.* The description of a tree is itself recursive – we cannot describe the children of a node without referring to the definition of a node. In other words, a node can have children, and those children are also nodes that can have children, and those children are also nodes, etc. etc. When we are dealing with a data structure that is fundamentally recursive, like a taxonomic tree, we shouldn't be surprised to find that the best ways to manipulate it also turn out to be recursive.

Recap

We started this chapter by comparing two different ways to generate lists of all possible DNA sequences of a given length. In doing so, we came across the idea of a *recursive function* – one that calls itself on a simpler version of the input. We saw that recursive functions have two important properties: a special condition under which they don't call themselves, and an assurance that the special condition will eventually be reached – usually when the simplification of the input reaches its limit. Using recursion to solve the kmer-generating problem revealed its tree-like structure.

We then looked at a couple of different ways of storing tree-like data in Python and discovered that, under the right circumstances, both parent → child and child → parent schemes can be useful[1]. We examined two common tree operations – finding lists of parents, and finding lists of

---
1   See the section on nested lists in the chapter on complex data structures for another way of storing tree data.

children – and showed how they can both be carried out using either iterative or recursive functions. Although we were investigating these operations in the context of taxonomic relationships, they are actually applicable to many different tree-like data types.

Exercise

Last Common Ancestor

A very common operation involving trees is identifying the Last Common Ancestor (LCA) of a group of nodes. In programming, we refer to the last common ancestor in a structural sense, rather than a biological one. For example, in our primates tree, the last common ancestor of *Pan troglodytes* and *Tarsius tarsier* is Haplorrhini.

Write a function that will take two arguments – a dictionary of child → parent relationships as described earlier in the chapter, and a list of taxa – and return the last common ancestor of the taxa. See if you can come up with both an iterative solution and a recursive one.

Hint: one approach to finding the last common ancestor of a list of taxa is as follows … find the last common ancestor of the first and second taxa and call that LC1. Then find the last common ancestor of LC1 and the third taxon and call that LC2. Then find the last common ancestor of LC2 and the fourth taxon etc. etc. The final last common ancestor will also be the last common ancestor of all the taxa in the list.

Solution

Last Common Ancestor

The hint gives us a pretty big clue that the solution to this problem is split into two parts: writing a function that will calculate the last common ancestor of any **two** given taxa, and then turning that into a function that will calculate the last common ancestor of a list of **any number** of taxa.

Let's tackle the two-taxon case first. A simple way to find the last common ancestor of two taxa is as follows: get a list of the parents of the first taxon, and a list of the parents of the second taxon, and then find the first taxon that occurs in both lists of parents.

Let's try an example from the tree of primates earlier in the chapter. Say we want to find the last common ancestor of *Pan troglodytes* and *Tarsius tarsier*. First we generate lists of parents for each of the two taxa. The parents of *Pan troglodytes* are

```
['Hominoidea', 'Simiiformes', 'Haplorrhini', 'Primates']
```

and the parents of *Tarsius tarsier* are

```
['Tarsiiformes', 'Haplorrhini', 'Primates']
```

Looking through both lists, we can see that the first taxon that occurs in both is 'Haplorrhini'.

Implementing this as a function is quite straightforward. We already have a function that returns a list of parents from earlier in the chapter, so we'll use that to generate the two lists of parents[1]. The easiest way to

---

1 It doesn't matter whether we use the iterative or recursive version.

Chapter 2: Recursion and trees

identify the first taxon that appears in both lists is to go through the second list one element at a time and return as soon as we find an element that's also in the first list:

```
def get_lca(taxon1, taxon2):
    taxon1_ancestors = [taxon1] + get_ancestors_rec(taxon1)
    for taxon in [taxon2] + get_ancestors_rec(taxon2):
        if taxon in taxon1_ancestors:
            return taxon
```

We'll check that it works by calling it with a couple of different pairs of taxa:

```
print(get_lca('Pan troglodytes','Tarsius tarsier'))
print(get_lca('Pan troglodytes','Pongo abelii'))
print(get_lca('Pan troglodytes','Strepsirrhini'))
```

and taking a look at the output:

```
Haplorrhini
Hominoidea
Primates
```

There are a couple of subtleties to getting the implementation just right. Note that the two input taxa don't have to have an equal number of parents – in the third function call we ask for the last common ancestor of a species (*Pan troglodytes*) and a suborder (Strepsirrhini) and the function still returns the correct answer. Also, we have to make sure that the list of ancestors to be considered for a taxon includes the taxon itself (hence the inclusion of the single-element list [taxon] in lines 2 and 3). That's necessary in order for the function to return the correct answer when one of the input taxa is a direct descendent of the other – for example `get_lca("Haplorrhini", "Pan troglodytes")`. The reason for this requirement will become clear soon!

Now for the interesting part – writing a function that uses the above function to find the last common ancestor for a list of taxa. As suggested in the problem description, we'll try both an iterative and a recursive solution. For the iterative solution, we'll remove taxa from the list one by one and repeatedly find the last common ancestor of the current taxon and the current last common ancestor. Here's the code for a function that implements this approach, along with a test function call:

```
def get_lca_list(taxa):
    taxon1 = taxa.pop()
    while len(taxa) > 0:
        taxon2 = taxa.pop()
        lca = get_lca(taxon1, taxon2)
        print('LCA of ' + taxon1 + ' and ' + taxon2 + ' is ' + lca)
        taxon1 = lca
    return taxon1

print(get_lca_list(['Pan troglodytes','Tarsius tarsier', 'Pongo abelii']))
```

get_lca_iterative.py

If we take a look at the output we can see what's happening:

```
LCA of Pongo abelii and Tarsius tarsier is Haplorrhini
LCA of Haplorrhini and Pan troglodytes is Haplorrhini
Haplorrhini
```

In the first iteration of the `while` loop, `taxon1` is `'Pongo abelii'` and `taxon2` is `'Tarsius tarsier'`[1]. We then use the `get_lca()` function defined previously to calculate the last common ancestor of these two taxa, and get the result `'Haplorrhini'`. This is assigned to the variable `taxon1`. Now we enter the second iteration of the `while` loop, remove the last (and only remaining) element from the taxon list (which is `'Pan troglodytes'`) and assign it to the variable `taxon2`.

---
1 Remember that the pop method takes the last element from a list.

Chapter 2: Recursion and trees

We use the `get_lca()` function to determine the last common ancestor of `'Haplorrhini'` and `'Pan troglodytes'`, which is `'Haplorrhini'`[1]. We assign this to `taxon1`. Now there are no remaining elements in the taxon list, the `while` loop ends and we return (and subsequently print) the value of `taxon1`, which for this function call is `'Haplorrhini'`.

Now let's try a recursive version. Just like with the previous examples, we'll need a plain English description to start with. How about this:

> *"To find the last common ancestor of a list of taxa, look at the size of the list. If there are only two taxa, then the answer is the last common ancestor of those two. If there are more than two, then remove the first taxon and call it taxon1, find the last common ancestor of the remaining items and call it taxon2, then the answer is the last common ancestor of taxon1 and taxon2."*

And here's the code:

```
def get_lca_list_rec(taxa):
    print("getting lca for " + str(taxa))
    if len(taxa) == 2:
        return get_lca(taxa[0], taxa[1])
    else:
        taxon1 = taxa.pop()
        taxon2 = get_lca_list_rec(taxa)
        return get_lca(taxon1, taxon2)
```

get_lca_recursive.py

Let's analyse how this function works in terms of the requirements for recursive functions that we saw earlier in the chapter. First, the special case: for this function, the special case (for which the function doesn't call itself) occurs when the list of taxa is has only two elements. For this

---

[1] This is the reason why our `get_lca` function has to work correctly when one of the arguments is also the result.

special case, we can find the last common ancestor of the list by using the existing `get_lca()` function. Second, the simplification process: for this function, the simplification takes place because one taxon is removed from the list at each function call. This guarantees that the special case will eventually be reached.

When looking at the solution code in the exercises folder, pay attention to the structure. There are three separate functions: one which calculates a list of ancestors for a single taxon, one which calculates the last common ancestor for a pair of taxa, and one which calculates the last common ancestor for a list of many taxa.

The two solutions we came up with above above show quite nicely the relative strengths and weaknesses of the iterative and recursive approaches. The recursive approach is easier to read and provides less scope for bugs, but the execution logic can be hard to follow if you're not used to recursion. The iterative approach, on the other hand, requires the programmer to carefully manage the taxon list. In the end, the choice of recursion or iteration to solve a given problem is in the hands of the programmer, and often comes down to how you feel more comfortable expressing the solution to a problem. Arguably, iterative programming involves telling the computer **how to find the solution** to a given problem, whereas recursive programming involves telling the computer **what the solution looks like**.

3: Complex data structures

In *Python for Biologists*, we spent quite a bit of time looking at different ways of storing data. Lists and dicts both had entire chapters devoted to them, and we used both dicts and lists extensively in the examples and exercises. For the material covered in this book, however, we need to dig a bit deeper into Python's data structures – in particular, we need to familiarize ourselves with the idea of complex data structures, and to introduce a few new types we haven't seen before.

Tuples

Tuples are a built in type of data structure that are part of the core Python distribution. At first glance, tuples appear very similar to lists – they have multiple elements, we can retrieve single element using square brackets, and we can iterate over the elements of a tuple. The only apparent difference is that we define them using parentheses rather than square brackets:

```
t = (4, 5, 6)
print t[1]
for e in t:
    print(e+1)
```
tuple.py

```
5
5
6
7
```

Our first clue about the role of tuples comes when we try to change one of the elements:

```
t[1] = 9
```

and are faced with an error:

```
TypeError: 'tuple' object does not support item assignment
```

The reason for this error is that a tuple cannot be changed once it has been created. Not only are we not allowed to change one of the elements, but we also can't append or remove elements, reverse or sort the elements, or carry out any other operation that changes the tuple. Data structures that have this property are said to be *immutable*[1].

It's not clear at first why this is a useful property to have – surely the point of variables is that they should be able to vary? But there are advantages to using tuples in some situations. Knowing that the value of a particular variable can't change after assignment can make it easier to reason about the behaviour of your code[2], and can allow Python to make certain optimizations which can sometimes result in faster or more memory-efficient code. Also, being immutable allows tuples to be used as the keys to a dict – something which is not possible with lists.

As a rule, tuples work well for *heterogeneous* data: sequences of elements which represent **different** bits of information, and where the **position** of each element tells you something about what the element stores. For example, here's a bit of code that creates a number of 3-element tuples to represent DNA sequence records. Each tuple stores a sequence, an accession number, and a genetic code, and they are always in the same order:

---

[1] Strings are also immutable in Python, which seems odd but doesn't generally cause problems.
[2] This is a similar idea to that of pure functions – see the chapter on functional programming for more discussion.

Chapter 3: Complex data structures

```
t1 = ('actgctagt', 'ABC123', 1)
t2 = ('ttaggttta', 'XYZ456', 1)
t3 = ('cgcgatcgt', 'HIJ789', 5)
```

It's often helpful to think of tuples as representing records, or rows from a table[1]. In contrast, lists are better for storing *homogeneous* data, where each element represents the same kind of thing. We'll encounter tuples elsewhere in this book and will use them, when appropriate, in examples.

Sets

A fairly frequent task in programming is to keep a list of items that share some common property. For example, imagine we are writing a program that processes a long list of accession numbers:

```
for acc in accessions:
    # do some processing
```

We suspect that our list `accessions` may contain duplicate elements. We want to avoid processing the same accession number multiple times, so we need to keep a record of which accession numbers have already been processed. We might be tempted to create a list to hold the processed accession numbers, and check it before processing each new one:

```
processed = []
for acc in accessions:
    if not acc in processed:
        # do some processing
        processed.append(acc)
```

The problem with this approach is that the operation of testing whether a particular value is in a list takes a long time if the list is large. The above

---

1   Or, if you're familiar with object oriented programming, lightweight immutable objects.

code will start out fast, but as the size of the `processed` list grows, so will the time required to check it on each iteration.

A faster alternative is to use a dict. We know that it's very quick to look up a value in a dict, so this approach will be much faster[1]:

```
processed = {}
for acc in accessions:
    if not acc in processed:
        # do some processing
        processed[acc] = 1
```

However, it's still not quite satisfactory – we are wasting a lot of memory storing all those values, all of which are 1, which we never look up.

Python's set type is like a dict that doesn't store any values – it simply stores a collection of keys and allows us to very rapidly check whether or not a particular key is in the set. Using a set is straightforward; we create an empty one using the `set()` function, add elements to it using `add()`, and check if a given element is in the set using `in()`:

```
processed = set()
for acc in accessions:
    if not acc in processed:
        # do some processing
        processed.add(acc)
```

We can also create a non-empty set by enclosing the elements in curly brackets:

```
set = {4,7,6,12}
```

Although this looks very similar to the way that we create a dict, it's easy to spot the difference – inside the brackets are individual elements, not key-value pairs.

---

[1] On my computer it's around one thousand times faster when `processed` holds a million elements.

Chapter 3: Complex data structures

Sets also have various useful methods for carrying out set operations like intersections, differences and unions, and can very quickly answer questions like "are all elements in my first set also in my second set?".

See the chapter on performance in *Effective Python development for biologists* for an in-depth look at the relative speed of lists and sets for different jobs.

Lists of lists

Let's look at a couple of examples of lists:

```
[1,2,3,4]
['a', 'b', 'c']
```

You've almost certainly encountered lists of numbers and strings like this in your programming so far. However, we're certainly not restricted to numbers and strings when constructing lists: we can make a list of file objects:

```
[open('one.txt'), open('two.txt')]
```

or a list of regular expression match objects:

```
import re
[re.search(r'[^ATGC]', 'ACTRGGT'), re.search(r'[^ATGC]', 'ACTYGGT')]
```

In fact, the elements of a list can be any type of value – including, interestingly, other lists:

```
[[1,2,3],[4,5,6],[7,8,9]]

# more readably
[[1,2,3],
 [4,5,6],
 [7,8,9]]
```

The data structure in the code above is a *list of lists*, sometimes known as a *two-dimensional list*. It may help to think of it like a table or a spreadsheet, where the elements of the outer list are rows, and the elements of the inner lists are cells. Although it looks weird, a list of lists behaves just like any other list. We can retrieve a single element using the normal syntax:

```
lol = [[1,2,3],[4,5,6],[7,8,9]]
print(lol[1])
# prints [4,5,6]
```

and then manipulate the returned list in exactly the same way:

```
lol = [[1,2,3],[4,5,6],[7,8,9]]
l = lol[1]
print(l[2])
# prints 6
```

We can also use a convenient shorthand to retrieve a single element directly from one of the inner lists: we just use two consecutive sets of square brackets:

```
lol = [[1,2,3],[4,5,6],[7,8,9]]
print(lol[1][2])
# prints 6
```

Multi-dimensional data structures are very useful in programming. Imagine storing a multiple sequence alignment as a list of lists:

```
aln = [['A', 'T', '-', 'T', 'G'],
       ['A', 'A', 'T', 'A', 'G'],
       ['T', '-', 'T', 'T', 'G'],
       ['A', 'A', '-', 'T', 'A']]
```

We can get an entire aligned sequence by retrieving a single element of the outer list:

Chapter 3: Complex data structures

```
seq = aln[2]
```

or get the character at a particular position using two sets of square brackets:

```
char = aln[2][3]
```

or get an entire column by retrieving a particular position for each inner row[1]:

```
col = [seq[3] for seq in aln]
```

Lists of dicts and lists of tuples

In a similar way, we can create lists of dicts and tuples. We can use lists of dicts or lists of tuples to store collections of related records – for example, here's our collection of DNA sequence records from earlier in the chapter stored as a list of dicts:

```
records = [
    {'name' : 'actgctagt', 'accession' : 'ABC123', 'genetic_code' : 1},
    {'name' : 'ttaggttta', 'accession' : 'XYZ456', 'genetic_code' : 1},
    {'name' : 'cgcgatcgt', 'accession' : 'HIJ789', 'genetic_code' : 5}
]
```

list_of_dicts.py

The dicts that make up the elements of this list are different from most of the ones we've seen before in two important ways. Firstly, they don't have names – in other words, they are not assigned to a variable (we call values like this *anonymous*, so each element of the list is an *anonymous dict*). This looks strange because we're used to storing dicts in variables, but in fact

---

1   Take a look at the chapter on generators for an explanation of this particular bit of syntax.

it's no stranger than the fact that the elements of the list [1,2,3] are *anonymous integers.*

Secondly, each value in one of the dicts above represents a different type of information – a DNA sequence, an accession number, and a genetic code – and they are a mixture of strings and numbers. In previous examples where we've used dicts, they've been storing pairs of data where each pair stores the same kind of thing – for example, restriction enzyme names and their cut motifs:

```
enzymes = {
    'EcoRI' : r'GAATTC',
    'AvaII' : r'GG(A|T)CC',
    'BisI'  : r'GC[ATGC]GC'
}
```

In the dicts that comprise the elements of our list, the data are stored very differently: the keys are simply labels which describe their values.

Just as with lists of lists, we can refer to an entire dict just by giving its index:

```
one_record = records[2]
```

but we're usually more interested in iterating over the dicts. The use of label-type keys leads to a very readable way of processing the dicts – for example, to print out the accession number and genetic code for each record:

```
for record in records:
    print('accession number : ' + record['accession'])
    print('genetic code: ' + str(record['genetic_code']))
```

list_of_dicts.py

Chapter 3: Complex data structures

```
accession number : ABC123
genetic code: 1
accession number : XYZ456
genetic code: 1
accession number : HIJ789
genetic code: 5
```

Recall from the earlier in the chapter that tuples are good for storing this kind of heterogeneous data. We could also store our collection of records using a list of tuples:

```
records = [
    ('actgctagt', 'ABC123', 1),
    ('ttaggttta', 'XYZ456', 1),
    ('cgcgatcgt', 'HIJ789', 5)
]
```

list_of_tuples.py

which avoids the need to store strings like `'accession'` multiple times, and instead relies on the ordering of the elements in each tuple to identify them. We can refer to individual elements of each tuple using the index:

```
for record in records:
    print('accession number : ' + record[1])
    print('genetic code: ' + str(record[2]))
```

Alternatively, a common idiom in Python is to assign all the elements of a tuple to temporary variables in one statement, then use those variables to refer to pieces of information from the current record:

```
for record in records:
    (this_sequence, this_accession, this_code) = record
    print('accession number : ' + this_accession)
    print('genetic code: ' + str(this_code))
```

list_of_tuples.py

This is known as *unpacking* the tuple, and leads to very readable code when the number of elements in the tuple is small.

Other complex structures

So far in this chapter we have mentioned four different types of collections (in Python these are known collectively as *sequences,* not to be confused with the DNA and proteins that we call sequences in biology): lists, tuples, dicts and sets. The mathematically-inclined reader will already have realized that for two-dimensional nested data structures there are sixteen possible combinations. Rather than run through all the possible variations (sets of dicts, tuples of lists, etc.) we will round out this chapter by concentrating on a few of the more useful ones. The rapid lookup of values from keys offered by dicts makes them very useful for nested data structures, so our last few examples will involves dicts of sets, tuples and lists, plus one more complex structure of particular interest to biologists: arbitrarily-nested lists.

Dicts of sets

When we are dealing with multiple sets in a program, storing them all in a dict offers a convenient way to label them without creating a bunch of extra variables. Imagine we have collected lists of genes (identified by accession numbers) that are over-expressed by some organism of interest when exposed to various types of heavy metal contaminants. We'll store the gene lists as a dict of sets, where the keys of the dict are the names of the heavy metals, and the values are the sets of genes[1]:

---

1 Obviously, in a real life analysis these would be created by reading the gene lists from a file rather than hard-coding them.

Chapter 3: Complex data structures

```
gene_sets = {
    'arsenic' : {1,2,3,4,5,6,8,12},
    'cadmium' : {2,12,6,4},
    'copper' : {7,6,10,4,8},
    'mercury' : {3,2,4,5,1}
}
```
dict_of_sets.py

This allows us to ask various questions: for example, is gene 3 over-expressed in response to arsenic?

```
3 in gene_sets['arsenic']
# True
```

Which conditions is gene 5 over-expressed in?

```
for metal, genes in gene_sets.items():
    if 5 in genes:
        print(metal)
```

---
mercury
arsenic
---

or more concisely using a list comprehension[1]:

```
print([metal for metal,gene_list in gene_sets.items() if 5 in gene_list])
# prints ['mercury', 'aresenic']
```

We can take advantage of set methods to do more sophisticated processing as well. The set method `issubset` will tell us whether one set is a subset of another – in other words, are all the elements in `set_one` also in `set_two`:

```
set_one.issubset(set_two)
```

[1] See the chapter on comprehensions for an explanation of this syntax

We can use two loops to iterate over our dict and carry out a pairwise comparison of our gene sets to identify conditions where all the over-expressed genes are also over-expressed in some other condition:

```
for condition1,set1 in gene_sets.items():
    for condition2,set2 in gene_sets.items():
        if set1.issubset(set2) and condition1 != condition2:
            print(condition1 + ' is a subset of ' + condition2)
```

dict_of_sets.py

```
mercury is a subset of arsenic
cadmium is a subset of arsenic
```

Dicts of tuples

Think back to the examples we looked at earlier in the chapter for storing a collection of DNA sequence records. We saw how these data could be stored using a list of tuples:

```
records = [
    ('actgctagt', 'ABC123', 1),
    ('ttaggttta', 'XYZ456', 1),
    ('cgcgatcgt', 'HIJ789', 5)
]
```

This approach worked well when we wanted to **iterate** over the records, but is not very good if we want to retrieve a **specific** record. Finding a record for which we know the accession number, for example, requires us to look at each record in turn until we find the one we want:

```
for record in records:
    if records[1] == 'XYZ456':
        # do something with the record
```

Chapter 3: Complex data structures

This is not only an extra chunk of typing, but the time required to carry out the search will grow linearly with the number of records.

If we know that we're frequently going to want to look up a record using a particular element – and, importantly, we are confident that element is unique to each record – we can store the data as a dict of tuples instead. To do this, we take the tuple element that uniquely identifies each record, and turn it into the key in a dict. The remaining tuple elements are the value:

```
records = {
    'ABC123' : ('actgctagt', 1),
    'XYZ456' : ('ttaggttta', 1),
    'HIJ789' : ('cgcgatcgt', 5)
}
```
dict_of_tuples.py

Now looking up the record for an accession is simply a matter of using the usual dict `get` method:

```
my_record = records.get('XYZ456')
```

and we can even combine this with tuple unpacking to achieve a very clear, readable syntax:

```
(my_sequence, my_code) = accession.get('XYZ456')
```

Dicts of lists

One of the frustrations that beginners tend to run into when using dicts is the restriction that keys must be unique. At first glance, this makes dicts seem a lot less useful than they ought to be, as often in programming we want rapid lookup of multiple values associated with a single key. Using

Chapter 3: Complex data structures

lists as the values in a dict offers a way round this restriction, and exposes the full usefulness of dicts.

Let's look at an example we've seen before in *Python for Biologists*: kmer counting. Previously, our goal has always been to count the number of times each kmer appears in a given DNA sequence, and we've usually ended up with a dict where the keys are the kmers and the values are the counts. But what if we're interested not just in the **number of times** a particular kmer occurs, but in the **positions** where it occurs? Let's remind ourselves of the standard way we're used to tackling this problem:

```
dna = 'aattggaattggaattg'
k = 4
kmer2count = {}
for start in range(len(dna) - k + 1):  ❶
    kmer = dna[start:start + k]  ❷
    current_count = kmer2count.get(kmer, 0)  ❸
    kmer2count[kmer] = current_count + 1  ❹

print(kmer2count)
```

In the above code we iterate over each possible start position using a range❶ and extract the kmer❷. We then look up the current count for that kmer from the dict❸, using a default value of zero if the kmer isn't already in the dict. Finally, we update the value in the dict for the kmer to be the current count plus one❹. We can see from the output that the result of running the code is a dict where the keys are kmers and the values are counts:

```
{'ggaa': 2, 'aatt': 3, 'tgga': 2, 'gaat': 2, 'attg': 3, 'ttgg': 2}
```

Modifying this code to store positions is quite straightforward. Rather than building up a dict where each value is a **count**, we will build up a dict where each value is a **list of start positions**. To do this, our default value

Chapter 3: Complex data structures

for a kmer that isn't currently in the dict will be an empty list, and rather than adding one to the count in each iteration, we'll append a position to the list:

```
dna = 'aattggaattggaattg'
k = 4
kmer2list = {}
for start in range(len(dna) - k + 1):
    kmer = dna[start:start + k]
    list_of_positions = kmer2list.get(kmer, [])
    list_of_positions.append(start)
    kmer2list[kmer] = list_of_positions
print(kmer2list)
```

dict_of_lists.py

As we can see from the output, what we end up with is a dict of lists:

```
{'ggaa': [4, 10], 'aatt': [0, 6, 12], 'gaat': [5, 11], 'tgga': [3, 9], 'attg': [1, 7, 13], 'ttgg': [2, 8]}
```

Notice how the order that the elements are stored in the dict bears no relation to the order of the start positions – remember, dicts have no inherent ordering. We can manipulate the items in the dict using standard tools, as long as we remember that every value is itself a list. For example, we can reconstruct our dict of kmer counts from the dict of start positions using a dict comprehension[1] which asks for the length of each start position list:

```
counts = {kmer: len(starts) for kmer, starts in kmer2list.items()}
```

---

1   See the chapter on comprehensions for a discussion of how this works.

Trees as nested lists

The data structures we've looked at so far in this chapter have all been two-dimensional: they have only two layers of collections before we reach the non-collection elements. It's perfectly possible to create higher-dimensional data structures in Python – lists of dicts of lists, sets of lists of tuples, etc. – but such structures are rarely helpful as they make it harder to think about the transformations that we want to apply to them. If, in the course of solving a programming problem, you find yourself reaching for a 3- or 4-dimensional data structure, then it's probably a good idea to encapsulate some of the complexity in an object.

There's one exception to this rule, though: arbitrarily nested lists offer quite a natural way to describe treelike data. Consider the standard Newick format[1] for representing phylogenetic trees:

```
(dog,(raccoon,bear),((sea_lion,seal),((monkey,cat),weasel)));
```

If we replace the parentheses with square brackets and put quotes around the names of the taxa, we get a valid bit of Python code that describes a nested set of lists:

```
['dog', ['raccoon','bear'], [['sea_lion','seal'],['monkey','cat'],
'weasel']]
```

Splitting the list definition over multiple lines doesn't change it, but makes it easier to read, and shows the tree-like structure a bit better:

---

1 http://evolution.genetics.washington.edu/phylip/newicktree.html

Chapter 3: Complex data structures

```
[
  'dog',
  [
    'raccoon','bear'
  ],
  [
    [
      'sea_lion','seal'
    ],
    [
      'monkey','cat'
    ],
    'weasel'
  ]
]
```

This particular tree is represented as a 3-dimensional list, and the internal structure is different from the other nested lists we have been looking at – the number of levels of nesting is different for different elements. The first element of the top-level list is a simple string (`'dog'`), the second element is a list (`['racoon', 'bear']`) and the third element is itself a nested list (`[['sea_lion','seal'], ['monkey','cat'], 'weasel']`).

This way of representing a tree has some interesting properties when compared with other approaches. To discuss them, we need to make extensive use of recursive functions, so make sure that you've read the chapter on recursion before reading the rest of this section.

Let's start by writing a recursive function to determine whether a particular subtree contains a given leaf node[1]:

---

[1] An alternative way to do this would be simply to flatten the list (i.e. turn it into a one-dimensional list) and look for the element.

```
def contains(my_list, target):
    result = False  ❶
    for element in my_list:
        if isinstance(element, list):  ❷
            if contains(element, target):
                result = True  ❸
        else:
            if element == target:
                result = True  ❸
    return result
```

leaf_in_subtree.py

We start off by defining a variable to hold the result, which will be `False` by default❶. The function then looks at each element in the input list and asks whether or not that element is itself a list using the `isinstance()` function❷. If it **is** a list, then it recursively calls itself on the element to check if it contains the target. If **not** then it determines whether the element is the target that we're looking for. If either of these possibilities is true, then we know that the list does contain the target, so the result is set to `True`❸. If it gets to the end of the input list without finding the target, then the result remains `False`. Either way, the value of `result` is returned.

Because the function is recursive we can use it on nested lists of any depth and elements of any type:

```
assert contains([1,2,3], 2)
assert contains([1,[2,3],[4,5], 5])
assert contains([['sea_lion','seal'],['monkey','cat'], 'weasel'], cat)
```

We can also use it to answer interesting phylogenetic questions. Here's a recursive function that iterates over all possible sublists of an input list (representing subtrees of a phylogenetic tree) and assembles a collection of all the sublists that contain two particular taxa:

Chapter 3: Complex data structures

```
def find_subtrees(my_list, taxon1, taxon2):
    result = []
    if contains(my_list, taxon1) and contains(my_list, taxon2):  ❶
        result.append(my_list)
    for sublist in my_list:  ❷
        if isinstance(sublist, list):
            result.extend(find_subtrees(sublist, taxon1, taxon2))  ❸
    return result
```

The way that the function works requires recursive thinking to understand. First it determines whether the input list contains both of the taxa❶ and, if so, adds it to a result list. Then it iterates over each element in the input list❷ and, if that element is itself a list, calls the `find_subtrees()` function recursively on it and adds the returned value to the result list❸.

The output of this function is a list, each element of which is a sublist of the input list. Here's an example – we'll ask for all the sublists of our tree that contain both `'monkey'` and `'cat'`:

```
tree = ['dog', ['raccoon','bear'], [['sea_lion','seal'],
['monkey','cat'], 'weasel']]
for subtree in find_subtrees(tree, 'monkey', 'cat'):
    print('subtree ' + str(subtree) + ' contains monkey and cat')
```

```
subtree ['dog', ['raccoon', 'bear'], [['sea_lion', 'seal'],
['monkey', 'cat'], 'weasel']] contains monkey and cat

subtree [['sea_lion', 'seal'], ['monkey', 'cat'], 'weasel']
contains monkey and cat

subtree ['monkey', 'cat'] contains monkey and cat
```

In programming terms, what we have done here is found a list of all the sublists that contain the strings `'monkey'` and `'cat'`. In phylogenetic terms, we have found a list of of the clades that contain these two organisms. Finding the smallest such clade is equivalent to identifying the last common ancestor of these two organisms, which we can do by writing another function which counts the number of leaf nodes in a subtree and using that function to sort[1] our list of subtrees:

```
def count_leaves(subtree):
    total = 0
    for element in subtree:
        if isinstance(element, list):
            total = total + count_leaves(element)
        else:
            total = total + 1
    return total

subtrees = find_subtrees(tree, 'monkey', 'cat')
sorted_subtrees = sorted(subtrees, key=count_leaves)
print(sorted_subtrees[0])
```

The first element of the sorted list of subtrees – the one with the fewest leaf nodes – is the smallest possible clade which contains our two taxa, and hence represents finding the last common ancestor of the two:

```
['monkey', 'cat']
```

Recap

This chapter has been all about ways of storing data: an introduction to two new data types and a discussion of complex data structures.

The new data types are intended for fairly specific uses, and you can get away without using for most programs – we can use lists instead of tuples, and dicts instead of sets – but having them in your toolbox leads to code that's more readable and robust. If you're used to programming with just lists and dicts, it might not be obvious when you encounter good

---

1 This use of sorting is discussed in the chapter on functional programming.

opportunities to use tuples and sets, so keep them at the back of your mind when writing code in future (hopefully the examples in the rest of this book will provide some inspiration).

Complex data structures are conceptually quite simple, but thinking and reasoning about them takes a bit of getting used to. We've seen in this chapter examples of the most common and useful types of complex data structures, involving lists, dicts, sets and tuples in various combinations. The examples that we've discussed illustrate an important point in programming: that picking the right representation for your data can make a big difference in how difficult it is to process them. Experience, along with exposure to real life examples, will make it clear to you which data structures are suitable for tackling which types of problems.

Exercises

Distance matrix

One of the questions we might want to ask of our heavy metal gene response data from earlier in the chapter is: which types of contamination provoke similar responses in expression levels? To answer it, we need to come up with a way of measuring how similar the sets of over-expressed genes are for any two give conditions. A straightforward metric is to divide the number of genes shared between the two lists (the *intersection*) by the total number of genes in both lists (the *union*). Write a program that will start with a list of sets (use the heavy metal data as an example) and produce a pairwise similarity matrix stored in a dict of dicts – i.e. we should be able to get the similarity score for two conditions by writing something like:

```
score = similarity_matrix['arsenic']['cadmium']
```

Testing for monopyly

Write a function that uses a phylogenetic tree stored as nested lists and determines whether or not two taxa are more closely related to each other than either is to a third taxon. Assume the tree is rooted.

Chapter 3: Complex data structures

Solutions

Distance matrix

There are two parts to this problem: calculating the similarity scores and creating the dict to hold the results. It's quite easy to calculate the similarity score for a given pair of sets – the names of the methods we need to use (`union` and `intersection`) are helpfully mentioned in the problem description, so we just have to divide the number of elements in the intersection by the number of elements in the union[1]:

```
gene_sets = {
        'arsenic' : {1,2,3,4,5,6,8,12},
        'cadmium' : {2,12,6,4},
        'copper'  : {7,6,10,4,8},
        'mercury' : {3,2,4,5,1}
}

set1 = gene_sets['arsenic']
set2 = gene_sets['mercury']
similarity = len(set1.intersection(set2)) / len(set1.union(set2))
# similarity == 0.625
```

Iterating over all possible pairwise comparisons is likewise quite easy – we just use two nested `for` loops. Remember that each pair in the `gene_sets` dict consists of the **name** of a condition (the key) and a **set** of genes identifiers (the value) so the best way to do the iteration is using the `items` method. Here we print out all the similarity scores, using a condition to avoid comparing a set to itself:

---

1   Remembering, if we're using Python 2, to include `from __future__ import division`.

Chapter 3: Complex data structures

```
for condition1, set1 in gene_sets.items():
    for condition2, set2 in gene_sets.items():
        if condition1 != condition2:
            similarity = len(set1.intersection(set2)) / len(set1.union(set2))
            print(condition1, condition2, similarity)
```

```
('mercury', 'copper', 0.1111111111111111)
('mercury', 'arsenic', 0.625)
('mercury', 'cadmium', 0.2857142857142857)
('copper', 'mercury', 0.1111111111111111)
('copper', 'arsenic', 0.3)
...
```

Notice from the output that we are considering each pair in both direction (e.g. mercury vs. copper and copper vs. mercury). We could avoid this, but it doesn't matter for the purpose of this exercise and it might be handy to be able to look up similarity scores in either direction, so we'll leave it.

Next, we come to the problem of storing the results. It's tempting to think that we can just create an empty dict before we start our loops and add elements at each iteration:

```
similarity_scores = {}
for condition1, set1 in gene_sets.items():
    for condition2, set2 in gene_sets.items():
        if condition1 != condition2:
            similarity = len(set1.intersection(set2)) / len(set1.union(set2))
            similarity_scores[condition1][condition2] = similarity
```

but this gives us a `KeyError`. The problem here is that the final line requires there to be a value associated with the key `condition1` in the `similarity_scores` dict, but we have never created one. Some programming languages (notably Perl) will automatically create keys in a

Chapter 3: Complex data structures

dict in these situations[1], but Python requires us to create the key ourselves. There are two approaches we can take – either we create a key for `condition1` at the start of the outer loop, and set the value to an empty dict❶:

```
similarity_scores = {}
for condition1, set1 in gene_sets.items():
    similarity_scores[condition1] = {}  ❶
    for condition2, set2 in gene_sets.items():
        if condition1 != condition2:
            similarity = len(set1.intersection(set2))/len(set1.union(set2))
            similarity_scores[condition1][condition2] = similarity
```

or we create a temporary dict at the start of the outer loop to hold the scores for the current iteration❶, and assign it to `condition1` at the end of the outer loop after it's been populated with scores❷:

```
similarity_scores = {}
for condition1, set1 in gene_sets.items():
    single_similarity = {}  ❶
    for condition2, set2 in gene_sets.items():
        if condition1 != condition2:
            similarity = len(set1.intersection(set2))/len(set1.union(set2))
            single_similarity[condition2] = similarity
    similarity_scores[condition1] = single_similarity  ❷
```
distance_matrix.py

Either way will work, and both will result in the same complex data structure being stored in `similarity_scores`:

---

1 This feature is called *autovivification*.

```
{'mercury':
   {'copper': 0.1111111111111111,
    'arsenic': 0.625,
    'cadmium': 0.2857142857142857},
 'copper':
   {'mercury': 0.1111111111111111,
    'arsenic': 0.3,
    'cadmium': 0.2857142857142857},
 'arsenic':
   {'mercury': 0.625,
    'copper': 0.3,
    'cadmium': 0.5},
 'cadmium':
   {'mercury': 0.2857142857142857,
    'copper': 0.2857142857142857,
    'arsenic': 0.5}
}
```

Given that this problem is all about transforming collections of data, we might wonder whether it's possible to express a solution in a functional programming style. The inner loop involves three elements: iterating over items in a dict, processing the items using some transformation, and a condition to ensure that only certain items get processed. The natural fit for this kind of job is a dict comprehension[1], and we can rewrite the inner loop to use one:

```
for condition1, set1 in gene_sets.items():
    single_scores = {
        condition2 : len(set1.intersection(set2))/len(set1.union(set2))
        for condition2,set2 in gene_sets.items()
        if condition1 != condition2
        }
    similarity_scores[condition1] = single_scores
```

In the above code, the dict comprehension has been split over multiple lines to make it easier to read, but it's a single Python statement. Whether you consider the procedural version or the comprehension version easier to read is a matter of personal preference and background.

---

1   See the chapter on comprehensions for a discussion of these.

Chapter 3: Complex data structures

We can even take things a step further and replace the outer `for` loop with another dict comprehension. Using two nested comprehensions in this way looks odd, but the key to reading it is to start with the innermost set of brackets. Using this approach we can transform our collection of gene sets into a collection of pairwise similarity scores in a single statement:

```
similarity_scores = {
    c1: {
        c2 : len(s1.intersection(s2)) / len(s1.union(s2))
        for c2,s2 in gene_sets.items()
        if c1 != c2
        }
    for c1,s1 in gene_sets.items()
}
```

Testing for monophyly

This exercise sounds quite difficult, but a lot of the hard work has already been done in the form of the functions that we examined earlier in the chapter. Recall that we already have a function for testing whether a given subtree contains a given taxon as one of its leaf nodes. A subtree supports the hypothesis that two taxa are more closely related to each other than either is to a third if it contains the first two taxa, but not the third – which we can test by using our `contains()` function in a complex condition:

```
if (contains(subtree, taxon1) and
    contains(subtree, taxon2) and not
    contains(subtree, taxon3)):
        # subtree supports closely related taxon1 + taxon2
```

Testing to see if a tree supports this hypothesis is just a question of asking if any of its subtrees fit the criterion of containing `taxon1` and `taxon2` but not `taxon3`. We can reuse most of the code for the function we saw earlier in the chapter to iterate over subtrees:

```
def are_closely_related(my_list, taxon1, taxon2, taxon3):
    result = False
    # does the current list match the condition?
    if (contains(my_list, taxon1)
    and contains(my_list, taxon2)
    and not contains(my_list, taxon3)):
        result = True
    # do any sublists match the condition?
    for sublist in my_list:
        if isinstance(sublist, list):
            if are_closely_related(sublist, taxon1, taxon2, taxon3):
                result = True
    return result

assert are_closely_related(tree, 'raccoon', 'dog', 'bear') == False
assert are_closely_related(tree, 'raccoon', 'bear', 'weasel') == True
assert are_closely_related(tree, 'raccoon', 'bear', 'dog') == True
```

monophyly.py

Instead of assembling a list of matching subtrees, here we're simply interested in a true-or-false answer, so we set the result to `False` initially, then change it to `True` if either the current nested list matches the condition or if any of the sublists match the condition. A few assertions test that the function works as expected.

4: object oriented Python

Introduction

If you've worked your way through *Python for Biologists*[1] you'll be vaguely aware that there are different "types" of things in Python – strings, numbers, files, regular expressions, etc. You may also have heard references to something called *object oriented programming*, which is often presented as a scary and esoteric technique that involves a lot of complicated-sounding concepts like *inheritance*, *composition*, and *polymorphism*. While it's true that there are many corners of the object oriented world which are daunting for the novice programmer, at its heart object oriented programming is simply the practice of **creating new types of things**.

In many ways, learning the tools of object oriented programming is much like learning to write functions. When we first learn to write small programs as complete beginners, we are content to use the built in functions and methods of Python as building blocks. Later, we learn to write our own functions, and find that this allows us to write larger and more complex programs more easily. It's the same with types: it's perfectly possible to write good and useful programs using only the types provided by the Python language, but learning how to create our own makes it much easier to solve a wide range of problems.

Indeed, the advantages of writing our own classes and writing our own functions are very similar. When we write our own functions, the basic building blocks that we have to use are the built in Python functions and methods. Writing our own functions doesn't allow us to do anything that we couldn't do before, it just allows us to structure our code in a way

---

[1] Or pretty much any other introductory Python book

that's much easier to read and write, and hence to write much larger and more sophisticated programs (think back to the concept of *encapsulation*). Similarly, learning to create our own types of object doesn't allow us to do anything fundamentally different – but it does let us structure code in a way that allows for much greater flexibility.

Before we dive in, a few sentences about nomenclature. So far, in both *Python for Biologists* and in this book, we've tended to use the word *type* to refer to the fact that values in Python come in different flavours, and the word *thing* to refer to a bit of data like a string or a file. For the purposes of this chapter, where our goal is to explicitly talk about objects, we are going to have to be a bit more precise. From now on, we will refer to an individual thing as an *object*, and the type of thing as its *class*. Instead of saying that a particular thing is of a particular type, we will say that a given *object* is an *instance* of a class. For example, in this line of code:

```
input = open("somedata.txt")
```

we will say that the `input` variable refers to an *object* that is an *instance* of the File *class*.

One common pitfall when learning about objects is getting confused about the difference between objects and classes, so I'll spell it out explicitly here. A *class* is like a blueprint for building objects. Defining a class doesn't cause any objects to be created directly, it simply describes what an instance of that class will look like when we do create it. Once we've defined a class, we can create as many *instances* – i.e. as many objects that use that class as a blueprint – as we like.

Some of the nomenclature for talking about classes we already know – for example, we know from *Python for Biologists* that a piece of code which belongs to objects of a particular class is a *method*.

Chapter 4: object oriented Python

A simple DNA sequence class

One of the tricky things about learning object oriented programming is that much of the value of doing so lies in the ability to create classes that solve **groups of related programming problems** rather than a **single, well-defined problem**. This leads to a slightly less straightforward learning experience than, for example, learning how to use loops. When learning to use loops, it's quite easy to show a problem that can't be solved without them, then present the solution, and get a very satisfying "Eureka!" moment. With object oriented programming we often have to use our imagination a bit more in order to see why various techniques are useful.

As an introduction to object oriented thinking, we'll take a look at a small collection of useful functions and see how we can use them to build up a set of classes for working with biological sequences.

Here are two useful functions for working with DNA sequences:

```
def get_AT(my_dna):
    length = len(my_dna)
    a_count = my_dna.count('A')
    t_count = my_dna.count('T')
    at_content = (a_count + t_count) / length
    return at_content

def complement(my_dna):
    replacement1 = my_dna.replace('A', 't')
    replacement2 = replacement1.replace('T', 'a')
    replacement3 = replacement2.replace('C', 'g')
    replacement4 = replacement3.replace('G', 'c')
    return replacement4.upper()
```

two_functions.py

Chapter 4: object oriented Python

The `get_AT()` function returns the AT content of the `my_dna` argument, and the `complement()` function returns the complement. Here's a very simple program that calls these two functions and prints out the results:

```
dna_sequence = "ACTGATCGTTACGTACGAGTCAT"
print(get_AT(dna_sequence))
print(complement(dna_sequence))
```

The output shows that the functions work as intended:

```
0.5652173913043478
TGACTAGCAATGCATGCTCAGTA
```

What if we want to attach a bit of metadata to the sequence – for example, the name of the gene, and the species to which it belongs? We can easily create a couple of new variables when we're dealing with just one sequence:

```
dna_sequence = "ACTGATCGTTACGTACGAGTCAT"
species = "Drosophila melanogaster"
gene_name = "ABC1"
print("Looking at the " + species " " + gene_name + " gene")
print("AT content is " + str(get_AT(dna_sequence)))
print("complement is " + complement(dna_sequence))
```

two_functions.py

But this obviously will not scale. To store a large collection of sequences along with their gene names and species names requires a different approach. We could create two dictionaries – one to store sequences and gene names, and one to store sequences and species names. But what if we want to store two sequences that are the same, but belong to different species? The dictionary approach won't work, since keys have to be unique. And it seems unlikely that we're going to want to look up the gene

Chapter 4: object oriented Python

name for a given sequence anyway – if anything, it's likely to be the other way round.

What we need in order to solve this problem elegantly is a way of wrapping up all three bits of information – the sequence, gene name, and species name – into one big ball of data which can be treated as a unit. One way to do this is with a complex data structure – for example, a list of dictionaries[1], where each dictionary represents a single sequence record and has three items corresponding to the three bits of information we need to store. A much better way is to create a *class* that represents a DNA sequence, instances of which can be created and passed around in our programs as discrete objects.

Defining a class is straightforward, but first we have to decide what instance variables and methods it will have. Instance variables are variables that belong to a particular object (we'll see how to use them soon). We already know what methods are – we've been using them on many of the built in Python classes. We want our class to have three instance variables (a DNA sequence, a gene name, and a species name) and two methods (the ones we saw previously: `getAT()` and `complement()`). For this example, our three instance variables are going to be strings, but they could also be File objects, dicts, lists, etc.

Here's a bit of code that defines our new class, creates an instance, and calls some methods on it:

---

1   Take a look at the chapter on complex data structures for some examples of this approach.

Chapter 4: object oriented Python

```
class DNARecord(object):
    sequence = 'ACGTAGCTGACGATC' ❶
    gene_name = 'ABC1'
    species_name = 'Drosophila melanogaster'

    def complement(self): ❷
        replacement1 = self.sequence.replace('A', 't')
        replacement2 = replacement1.replace('T', 'a')
        replacement3 = replacement2.replace('C', 'g')
        replacement4 = replacement3.replace('G', 'c')
        return replacement4.upper()

    def get_AT(self): ❸
        length = len(self.sequence)
        a_count = self.sequence.count('A')
        t_count = self.sequence.count('T')
        at_content = (a_count + t_count) / length
        return at_content

d = DNARecord() ❹
print('Created a record for ' + d.gene_name + ' from ' + d.species_name)
print('AT is ' + str(d.get_AT()))
print('complement is ' + d.complement())
```

dna_record.py

There's a lot going on in this code sample, so we'll go through it line by line.

We start with the keyword `class`, followed by the name of our class with the name of the base class in parentheses (don't worry for now about the meaning of the base class, we will discuss it later). This line ends with a colon and, as we might expect, the rest of the class definition is indented.

On the next few lines❶ we define some attributes of the class – a DNA sequence, a gene name and a species name.

Next, we start defining our first method – the `complement()` method❷. The method definition works just like a function definition, except that it takes as its first argument a special variable called `self`[1]. This `self`

---
1 Java programmers will be familiar with the concept as `this`.

Chapter 4: object oriented Python

variable is how we refer to the object inside the method – so, to refer to the DNA sequence of the record, we use the variable name `self.sequence`. We don't have to worry about how the `self` variable gets created – Python automatically takes care of setting the value of the `self` variable whenever we make a method call on our object. We make use of the `self` variable again in the `get_AT()` method❸.

The next few lines of code are where we start to use our new class. We create a new instance of our `DNARecord` class by writing the name of the class followed by a pair of parentheses (we'll learn more about the reason for these shortly)❹. Once the new object has been created, and assigned to the variable `d`, we can access its attributes using the pattern `variablename.attributename`. So to get the gene name of the `DNARecord` referred to by the variable `d`, we simply write `d.gene_name`. To call a method on our new object, we use the same pattern.

Now we've seen what a class definition looks like, let's see what can be done to improve it.

Constructors

An obvious limitation of the class as we've written it above is that the three members – `sequence`, `gene_name` and `species_name` – are set as part of the class definition. This means that every instance of this class we create will have the same values set for these variables, which is unlikely to be useful. Of course, once we've created an object we can change its member variables, so if we want two different DNA records with different properties then we can simply set them after the objects have been created:

```
d1 = DNARecord()
d1.sequence = 'ATATATTATTATATTATA'
d1.gene_name = 'COX1'
d1.species_name = 'Homo sapiens'

d2 = DNARecord()
d2.sequence = 'CGGCGGCGCGGCGCGGCG'
d2.gene_name = 'ATP6'
d2.species_name = 'Gorilla gorilla'

for r in [d1, d2]:
    print('Created ' + r.gene_name + ' from ' + r.species_name)
    print('AT is ' + str(r.get_AT()))
    print('complement is ' + r.complement())
```

We're using the exact same class definition as above, but this time after creating each **DNARecord** object we set it's properties, before using a loop to iterate over the two records and print their information. We can see from the output how the updated values for the member variables are used when we ask for the AT content or for the complement:

```
Created COX1 from Homo sapiens
AT is 1
complement is TATATAATAATATAATAT
Created ATP6 from Gorilla gorilla
AT is 0
complement is GCCGCCGCGCCGCGCCGC
```

Note that when we update a member variable of an instance of an object, it only affect that particular instance – when we set the sequence for **d1**, it doesn't affect **d2**, or any other **DNARecord** objects that might be created.

Looking at the above code, it's clear that we are often going to want to set all the variables of an object in one go. In the above code we do this in three separate statements, but we might be tempted to make life easier by

Chapter 4: object oriented Python

creating another method for our object whose job is to set its variables. Here's what it might look like:

```python
class DNARecord(object):
    sequence = 'ACGTAGCTGACGATC'
    gene_name = 'ABC1'
    species_name = 'Drosophila melanogaster'

    def complement(self):
        ...

    def get_AT(self):
        ...

    def set_variables(self, new_seq, new_gene_name, new_species_name):  ❶
        self.sequence = new_seq
        self.gene_name = new_gene_name
        self.species_name = new_species_name

d1 = DNARecord()
d1.set_variables('ATATATTATTATATTATA','COX1','Homo sapiens')  ❷

d2 = DNARecord()
d2.set_variables('CGGCGGCGCGGCGCGGCG','ATP6','Gorilla gorilla')  ❷

for r in [d1, d2]:
    print('Created ' + r.gene_name + ' from ' + r.species_name)
    print('AT is ' + str(r.get_AT()))
    print('complement is ' + r.complement())
```

set_variables.py

The new method❶ follows the normal rule for object methods – the first argument is `self` – and sets the three variables using the remaining arguments. Later we can see how this method allows us to set all the variables in one statement❷.

Now that we've made it so easy to set the variables, there's no need to have them as part of the class definition, so we can tidy up our class by removing them. Everything will still work fine as long as we remember to set the variables for an object after we create it:

```
class DNARecord(object):

    def complement(self):
        ...

    def get_AT(self):
        ...

    def set_variables(self, new_seq, new_gene_name, new_species_name):
        self.sequence = new_seq
        self.gene_name = new_gene_name
        self.species_name = new_species_name
d1 = DNARecord()
d1.set_variables('ATATATTATTATATTATA','COX1','Homo sapiens')

d2 = DNARecord()
d2.set_variables('CGGCGGCGCGGCGCGGCG','ATP6','Gorilla gorilla')

for r in [d1, d2]:
    print('Created ' + r.gene_name + ' from ' + r.species_name)
    print('AT is ' + str(r.get_AT()))
    print('complement is ' + r.complement())
```

However, this allows us to get into difficulties if we accidentally try to use a newly created object before its variables have been set:

```
d1 = DNARecord()
print(d1.complement())
```

The above code will give us an error letting us know that Python can't find the sequence in order to calculate the complement:

```
Traceback (most recent call last):
    replacement1 = self.sequence.replace('A', 't')
AttributeError: 'DNARecord' object has no attribute 'sequence'
```

Chapter 4: object oriented Python

To avoid running into this problem, Python[1] has a special kind of method called a *constructor*. The job of a constructor is to create a new object and set its variables all in one statement, and it uses a bit of special syntax:

```
class DNARecord(object):

    def __init__(self, sequence, gene_name, species_name):❶
        self.sequence = sequence
        self.gene_name = gene_name
        self.species_name = species_name

    def complement(self):
        ...
    def get_AT(self):
        ...

d1 = DNARecord('ATATATTATTATATTATA', 'COX1', 'Homo sapiens')❷
print(d1.complement())
```
constructor.py

The constructor method❶ has an unusual name – two underscores, followed by the word `init`, followed by another two underscores. This special name tells Python that this isn't just another ordinary method, but one that has a special job. Notice that when we create our **DNARecord** object❷ we simply pass in the values we want our new object to have as arguments to **DNARecord()**. Python takes care of creating the object, running the **__init__()** method, and returning the newly created object all in one go. Now, if we try to create a **DNARecord** object without telling Python what we want it's member variables to be:

```
d2 = DNARecord()
```

We will get an error right away:

---

1   And other object oriented languages.

```
TypeError: __init__() takes exactly 4 arguments (1 given)
```

It's worth pausing at this point and comparing the object oriented code we get when using the class definition above with the imperative style code we saw at the start of the chapter:

```
# imperative code
dna_sequence = "ACTGATCGTTACGTACGAGT"
species = "Drosophila melanogaster"
gene_name = "ABC1"
print("Looking at the " + species + " " + gene_name + " gene")
print("AT content is " + get_AT(dna_sequence))
print("complement is " + complement(dna_sequence))

# object oriented code
d1 = DNARecord("ACTGATCGTTACGTACGAGT", "ABC1", "Drosophila melanogaster")
print("Looking at the " + d1.species_name + " " + d1.gene_name + " gene")
print("AT content is " + str(d1.get_AT()))
print("complement is " + d1.complement())
```

Notice the difference in *how the data are stored*, and *how they are processed*. In the imperative code, we create three variables to hold the three bits of data, and then pass them to the functions to get the answers we want. In the object oriented style, we package up the three bits of data into one object, then ask the object for the answers we want. The object is responsible for both storing its own variables, and calculating the AT and complement. In other words, when we want to know the AT content of a `DNARecord` object, we don't ask for the sequence and then pass it to a function, we simply ask for the AT content directly, and it's the object's job to tell us.

Once we've defined a new class, it behaves just the same as a built in class – there's no difference in how we use a `DNARecord` object compared to a `File` object or a `String` object or an `Integer` object. We can store a

Chapter 4: object oriented Python

DNARecord object in a variable, list or dict; we can pass it as an argument to a function or method, and we can return it from a function or method. For example, here's a function that takes a **DNARecord** as an argument and returns the protein translation as a string[1]:

```
def translate_dna(dna_record):
    gencode = {
        'ATA':'I', 'ATC':'I', 'ATT':'I', 'ATG':'M',
        'ACA':'T', 'ACC':'T', 'ACG':'T', 'ACT':'T',
        'AAC':'N', 'AAT':'N', 'AAA':'K', 'AAG':'K',
        'AGC':'S', 'AGT':'S', 'AGA':'R', 'AGG':'R',
        'CTA':'L', 'CTC':'L', 'CTG':'L', 'CTT':'L',
        'CCA':'P', 'CCC':'P', 'CCG':'P', 'CCT':'P',
        'CAC':'H', 'CAT':'H', 'CAA':'Q', 'CAG':'Q',
        'CGA':'R', 'CGC':'R', 'CGG':'R', 'CGT':'R',
        'GTA':'V', 'GTC':'V', 'GTG':'V', 'GTT':'V',
        'GCA':'A', 'GCC':'A', 'GCG':'A', 'GCT':'A',
        'GAC':'D', 'GAT':'D', 'GAA':'E', 'GAG':'E',
        'GGA':'G', 'GGC':'G', 'GGG':'G', 'GGT':'G',
        'TCA':'S', 'TCC':'S', 'TCG':'S', 'TCT':'S',
        'TTC':'F', 'TTT':'F', 'TTA':'L', 'TTG':'L',
        'TAC':'Y', 'TAT':'Y', 'TAA':'_', 'TAG':'_',
        'TGC':'C', 'TGT':'C', 'TGA':'_', 'TGG':'W'}
    last_codon_start = len(dna_record.sequence) - 2
    protein = ""
    for start in range(0,last_codon_start,3):
        codon = dna_record.sequence[start:start+3]
        aa = gencode.get(codon.upper(), 'X')
        protein = protein + aa
    return protein
```

translate_record.py

Inheritance

What other useful methods could we add to our **DNARecord** class? How about a method which returns the record in FASTA format. We'll combine the **gene_name** and **species_name** member variables to construct the

---

[1] See the *dictionaries* chapter in *Python for Biologists* for a reminder of how this function works.

Chapter 4: object oriented Python

header, replacing any spaces in the species name with underscores[1]. add a greater-than symbol at the start, and separate the header and sequence with a newline character[2]:

```
class DNARecord(object):

    def __init__(self, sequence, gene_name, species_name):
        ...
    def complement(self):
        ...
    def get_AT(self):
        ...

    def get_fasta(self):
        safe_species_name = self.species_name.replace(' ','_')
        header = '>' + self.gene_name + '_' + safe_species_name
        return header + '\n' + self.sequence + '\n'
```

fasta_method.py

A quick check will allow us to make sure that the method's working as expected:

```
d1 = DNARecord('ATATATTATTATATTATA', 'COX1', 'Homo sapiens')
print(d1.get_fasta())
```

```
>COX1_Homo_sapiens
ATATATTATTATATTATA
```

We now have a **DNARecord** object that can do **three** useful things – calculate its AT content, calculate its complement, and generate a FASTA format string. We can write programs to carry out simple bioinformatics tasks using this object. For example, if we have a list of **DNARecord**

---

1 Some sequence analysis tools are fussy about not allowing spaces in FASTA headers.
2 We also add another newline character at the end so that we can create a multi-sequence FASTA file simply by writing the result of several **get_fasta()** method calls consecutively.

Chapter 4: object oriented Python

objects, we can generate a FASTA file containing just the sequences with a high AT content:

```
output = open("high_at.fasta", "w")
for d in my_dna_records:
    if d.get_AT() > 0.6:
        output.write(d.get_fasta())
```

Now that we've seen how useful objects can be, we might want to create a similar class to represent a protein record – let's call it `ProteinRecord` for consistency. Just like the `DNARecord` class, it will have a `gene_name`, a `species_name`, and a `sequence`. What methods should our `ProteinRecord` class have? Obviously it doesn't make any sense to ask for the complement of a protein sequence, or to ask for its AT content. Instead, we'll give it a method that calculates the proportion of the amino acid residues that are hydrophobic[1]. We'll also include the method that generates the FASTA sequence – since DNA and protein FASTA formats look the same, we can just reuse our `get_fasta()` method.

Here's a first attempt at the code for our `ProteinRecord` class:

---

[1] Take a look at the exercise in the chapter of *Python for Biologists* on writing our own functions for a discussion of how this method works.

```
class ProteinRecord(object):

    def __init__(self, sequence, gene_name, species_name):
        self.sequence = sequence
        self.gene_name = gene_name
        self.species_name = species_name

    def get_fasta(self):
        safe_species_name = self.species_name.replace(' ','_')
        header = '>' + self.gene_name + '_' + safe_species_name
        return header + '\n' + self.sequence + '\n'

    def get_hydrophobic(self):
        aa_list=['A','I','L','M','F','W','Y','V']
        protein_length = len(self.sequence)
        total = 0
        for aa in aa_list:
            aa = aa.upper()
            aa_count = self.sequence.count(aa)
            total = total + aa_count
        percentage = total * 100 / protein_length
        return percentage
```

protein_record.py

There's nothing going on here that's particularly different to what we had in our **DNARecord** class. We still have a constructor that handles the job of setting the instance variables and the same **get_fasta()** method that handles the job of creating a FASTA format string. We also have the new **get_hydrophobic()** method whose job is to calculate the percentage of hydrophobic residues in the sequence. Here's a few lines of code showing how everything works:

```
d1 = ProteinRecord('MSRSLLLRFLLFLLLLPPLP', 'COX1', 'Homo sapiens')
print(d1.get_fasta())
print(str(d1.get_hydrophobic()))
```

And here's the output:

Chapter 4: object oriented Python

```
>COX1_Homo_sapiens
MSRSLLLRFLLFLLLLPPLP
```

Everything seems to be working perfectly. The only thing that feels slightly unsatisfactory is that we have the exact same `get_fasta()` code duplicated in both the `DNARecord` and `ProteinRecord` class definitions. This feels wrong; we know from previous experience that code reuse is a Good Thing, and that having the exact same code defined in two places is a Bad Thing. We could get round this by moving the `get_fasta()` code to a method outside the class definitions and have it called by the classes, but that would break the encapsulation – the objects would no longer be responsible for generating their own FASTA sequence.

The key to resolving this problem is to take advantage of an object oriented feature called *inheritance*. Inheritance allows two different classes – in our case, `DNARecord` and `ProteinRecord` – to share code. The way it works is quite straightforward: we create a third class to hold the shared code, and then tell Python that the two classes should inherit methods from it. This third class is called the *superclass* (or *base class*) of the other two, and the other two are called *subclasses* (or *derived classes*) of the third one. We'll call our third class `SequenceRecord`, and it will hold the methods (`__init__()` and `get_fasta()`) that are common to both `DNARecord` and `ProteinRecord`:

Chapter 4: object oriented Python

```
class SequenceRecord(object):

    def __init__(self, sequence, gene_name, species_name):
        self.sequence = sequence
        self.gene_name = gene_name
        self.species_name = species_name

    def get_fasta(self):
        safe_species_name = self.species_name.replace(' ','_')
        header = '>' + self.gene_name + '_' + safe_species_name
        return header + '\n' + self.sequence + '\n'
```

inheritance.py

So far, so familiar: `SequenceRecord` is just another class definition. But here's where it gets interesting – we'll rewrite the class definitions of `DNARecord` and `ProteinRecord` so that they inherit from this class. To do this, we just change the content of the parentheses after `DNARecord` in the class definition to `SequenceRecord`, and include only the methods that we want to belong just to our `DNARecord` class – `complement()` and `get_AT()`:

```
class DNARecord(SequenceRecord):

    def complement(self):
        ...

    def get_AT(self):
        ...
```

inheritance.py

Likewise, for the `ProteinRecord` class definition we supply the name of the superclass – `SequenceRecord` – and the definition of the `get_hydrophobic()` function:

Chapter 4: object oriented Python

```
class ProteinRecord(SequenceRecord):

    def get_hydrophobic(self):
        ...
```

inheritance.py

Let's look at where this leaves us. We have one base class – `SequenceRecord` – which holds the methods (the `__init__()` constructor and `get_fasta()`) which are common to both sequence types. Then we have two subclasses – `DNARecord` and `ProteinRecord` – that inherit these methods, and add their own. Let's look at the object oriented code in full:

```
class SequenceRecord(object):

    def __init__(self, sequence, gene_name, species_name):
        self.sequence = sequence
        self.gene_name = gene_name
        self.species_name = species_name

    def get_fasta(self):
        safe_species_name = self.species_name.replace(' ','_')
        header = '>' + self.gene_name + '_' + safe_species_name
        return header + '\n' + self.sequence + '\n'

class ProteinRecord(SequenceRecord):

    def get_hydrophobic(self):
        aa_list=['A','I','L','M','F','W','Y','V']
        protein_length = len(self.sequence)
        total = 0
        for aa in aa_list:
            aa = aa.upper()
            aa_count = self.sequence.count(aa)
            total = total + aa_count
        return total * 100 / protein_length

class DNARecord(SequenceRecord):

    def complement(self):
        replacement1 = self.sequence.replace('A', 't')
        replacement2 = replacement1.replace('T', 'a')
        replacement3 = replacement2.replace('C', 'g')
        replacement4 = replacement3.replace('G', 'c')
        return replacement4.upper()

    def get_AT(self):
        length = len(self.sequence)
        a_count = self.sequence.count('A')
        t_count = self.sequence.count('T')
        return (a_count + t_count) / length
```

inheritance.py

The benefit of structuring things in this way is that all our methods are only defined once, but can be used by all the appropriate classes, allowing us to easily mix and match different sequence types in a script:

```
p1 = ProteinRecord('MSRSLLLRFLLFLLLLPPLP', 'COX1', 'Homo sapiens')
print(p1.get_fasta())
print(p1.get_hydrophobic())

d1 = DNARecord('ATCGCGTACGTGATCGTAG', 'COX1', 'Homo sapiens')
print(d1.get_fasta())
print(d1.complement())
```

Notice how in this example, we only ever create instances of the subclasses – **DNARecord** and **ProteinRecord**. We never create an instance of **SequenceRecord** directly[1]. By way of illustration, here's a modified version of our translation function that takes a **DNARecord** as its argument and returns a **ProteinRecord**:

---

[1] Although there is nothing to stop us doing so.

```
def translate_dna(dna_record):
    gencode = {
        'ATA':'I', 'ATC':'I', 'ATT':'I', 'ATG':'M',
        'ACA':'T', 'ACC':'T', 'ACG':'T', 'ACT':'T',
        'AAC':'N', 'AAT':'N', 'AAA':'K', 'AAG':'K',
        'AGC':'S', 'AGT':'S', 'AGA':'R', 'AGG':'R',
        'CTA':'L', 'CTC':'L', 'CTG':'L', 'CTT':'L',
        'CCA':'P', 'CCC':'P', 'CCG':'P', 'CCT':'P',
        'CAC':'H', 'CAT':'H', 'CAA':'Q', 'CAG':'Q',
        'CGA':'R', 'CGC':'R', 'CGG':'R', 'CGT':'R',
        'GTA':'V', 'GTC':'V', 'GTG':'V', 'GTT':'V',
        'GCA':'A', 'GCC':'A', 'GCG':'A', 'GCT':'A',
        'GAC':'D', 'GAT':'D', 'GAA':'E', 'GAG':'E',
        'GGA':'G', 'GGC':'G', 'GGG':'G', 'GGT':'G',
        'TCA':'S', 'TCC':'S', 'TCG':'S', 'TCT':'S',
        'TTC':'F', 'TTT':'F', 'TTA':'L', 'TTG':'L',
        'TAC':'Y', 'TAT':'Y', 'TAA':'_', 'TAG':'_',
        'TGC':'C', 'TGT':'C', 'TGA':'_', 'TGG':'W'}
    last_codon_start = len(dna_record.sequence) - 2
    protein = ""
    for start in range(0,last_codon_start,3):
        codon = dna_record.sequence[start:start+3]
        aa = gencode.get(codon.upper(), 'X')
        protein = protein + aa

    # gather the information to create the protein record
    protein_name = dna_record.gene_name
    protein_species = dna_record.species_name

    # create the protein record and return it
    protein_record = ProteinRecord(protein,protein_name,protein_species)

    return protein_record
```

Overriding

Occasionally we'll want a subclass to behave in a slightly different way to its superclass – the mechanism that allows us to do this is called *overriding*. Suppose that we want our **DNARecord** objects to have a **genetic_code** variable, which stores the number of the genetic code for

Chapter 4: object oriented Python

the sequence using the NCBI numbering scheme[1]. We cannot simply add this variable to the constructor for the `SequenceRecord` class, as it doesn't make sense to have a genetic code for a protein sequence. Instead, what we need to do is supply the `DNARecord` class with its very own, specialized constructor, which will take a genetic code as one of its arguments. That way, when we create a new `DNARecord` object the `__init__()` method defined in `DNARecord` will be used, but when we call `get_fasta()` on the object, it will still use the method defined in `SequenceRecord`. Let's look at the code:

```
class DNARecord(SequenceRecord):

    def __init__(self, sequence, gene_name, species_name, genetic_code):

        self.sequence = sequence
        self.gene_name = gene_name
        self.species_name = species_name
        self.genetic_code = genetic_code

    def complement(self):
        ...

    def get_AT(self):
        ...
```

overriding.py

We can now create `DNARecord` objects using four initial variables – a gene name, a species name, a sequence, and a genetic code:

```
d1 = DNARecord('ATCGCGTACGTGATCGTAG', 'COX1', 'Homo sapiens', 5)
print(d1.get_fasta())
print(d1.complement())
print('genetic code is ' + str(d1.genetic_code))
```

The definition of the `__init__()` method in `DNARecord` is said to *override* the one in `SequenceRecord`. Of course, it's not just constructors

---
1 http://www.ncbi.nlm.nih.gov/Taxonomy/Utils/wprintgc.cgi

that can be overridden in this way – we can do the same for any method.

Calling methods in the superclass

The above example is straightforward, because we wanted to entirely replace the superclass method with a new one. What if instead, we wanted to add a bit of functionality? For example, imagine that we decide to add a bit of error-checking to the `SequenceRecord` constructor. We would like to make sure that the species name provided in the constructor arguments really does look like a species name. It should have two parts separated by a space, and the first part should start with a capital letter. We can write a regular expression to describe this pattern[1], and then if the given species name doesn't match it, exit the program with an error message[2]. Here's the code:

```
import re

class SequenceRecord(object):

    def __init__(self, sequence, gene_name, species_name):
        if not re.match(r'[A-Z][a-z]+ [a-z]+', species_name):
            exit(species_name + ' is not a valid species name!')
        self.sequence = sequence
        self.gene_name = gene_name
        self.species_name = species_name

    def get_fasta(self):
        ...
```

This works fine, but we run into a problem – we would like this functionality to be shared by all subclasses of `SequenceRecord` (i.e. both `DNARecord` and `ProteinRecord`). However, recall that we just added a specialized constructor for `DNARecord` in order to allow it to

---
1   See the regular expressions chapter in *Python for Biologists* if you need a refresher.
2   There is a much better way to handle this type of situation, which we will learn about in the chapter on exceptions.

have a genetic code. When we create a new instance of DNARecord, it is the specialized constructor that runs, not the one in SequenceRecord, so DNARecord can't take advantage of this useful species name checking functionality.

What we would really like to be able to do is to call the SequenceRecord constructor from inside the DNARecord constructor, and only then add on the extra genetic_code variable. Fortunately, Python has a built in mechanism to allow this – we can call the SequenceRecord constructor directly by calling SequenceRecord.__init__(). Here's how it works in practice:

```
class DNARecord(SequenceRecord):

    def __init__(self, sequence, gene_name, species_name, genetic_code):
        # first call the SequenceRecord constructor to check the species name
        SequenceRecord.__init__(self, sequence, gene_name, species_name)
        # now set the genetic code
        self.genetic_code = genetic_code

    def complement(self):
        ...

    def get_AT(self):
        ...
```

calling_superclass.py

Now we have the best of both worlds. Our DNARecord class is able to take advantage of the improvements to the SequenceRecord constructor, and still implement its own specialized behaviour.

Polymorphism

Polymorphism is a complicated name for a simple concept: code that does different things depending on the type of data on which it's operating.

Here's a somewhat contrived example: imagine that we want to add a method to our sequence objects that will return the length of the protein sequence that they represent. Obviously we are going to need a different method for DNA and protein sequences – for protein sequences, we just need to return the length of the `sequence` variable, but for DNA sequences we need to return the length of the `sequence` variable divided by three. Because we need different methods for each type of sequence, we can't add the method to the `SequenceRecord` class definition, but must instead add it separately to both the `DNARecord` and `ProteinRecord` class definitions:

```
class ProteinRecord(SequenceRecord):

    def get_protein_length(self):
        return len(self.sequence)

    ...

class DNARecord(SequenceRecord):

    def get_protein_length(self):
        return len(self.sequence) / 3

    ...
```

Now suppose that we have a list of sequence records that are a mixture of DNA and protein sequences, and we want to do something to just the ones whose protein length is greater than one hundred amino acid residues. Rather than having to examine each record and check whether it is a `DNARecord` or a `ProteinRecord`, we can simply call the `get_protein_length` method on each, and Python will take care of making sure that the correct method is called:

Chapter 4: object oriented Python

```
for my_record in list_of_records:
    if my_record.get_protein_length() > 100:
        # do something with the record
```

We've actually encountered this type of behaviour before. Recall that we can iterate over an file, string or list using exactly the same syntax – this is an example of polymorphism.

Recap

object oriented programming is a big topic, and whole libraries of books have been written about its ramifications. In this chapter we've seen a brief overview of the ways that basic object oriented features work in Python. We've looked at how we can use simple class definitions to package data and code together in logical units which we can create and pass around in our programs. We've also seen how we can allow our classes to share functionality using *inheritance*, and how we can give them specialized behaviour by *overriding* methods in their base class. Finally, we've looked at one important benefit of object oriented thinking – the ability of functions to handle different types of data transparently.

Because object oriented programming is such a complex topic, there are many aspects worth reading up on that are beyond the scope of this book. *Composition* is an alternative to inheritance which also allows classes to share functionality, but in a different way. Unlike many languages, Python allows for *multiple inheritance*, an easily abused technique that allows classes to inherit from multiple parents. Much thought has been given to solving common abstract problems in an object oriented style and the result is *design patterns* – a set of best practise techniques that are applicable to many different languages and problems[1]. Finally, there are a

---

1   Though design patterns tend to be used less often in Python than in other languages as its dynamic nature makes many of them unnecessary.

few aspects of object oriented programming – *interfaces* and *abstract classes* – which don't really exist in Python but which are worth learning about.

Exercise

Write an object oriented program that simulates evolution at three loci in a population of one hundred haploid individuals[1]. Each locus has two alleles which differ slightly in fitness and the overall fitness for an individual can be calculated from the fitness of its three loci using a multiplicative model (i.e. if the fitness scores for the alleles of a given individual are 1, 0.9 and 0.8 then the individual's fitness is 1 * 0.9 * 0.8 = 0.72).

In every generation, the simulation proceeds in two stages. Firstly, to represent selection, each individual is potentially killed with a probability inversely proportional to the fitness – in other words, for each individual, pick a random number between 0 and 1 and if that number is greater than the individual's fitness, it dies and is removed from the population. Secondly, to represent reproduction, new individuals are added to the population to make the numbers back up to one hundred. Rather than simulating recombination etc. we will simply say that the alleles for each new individual are chosen by randomly selecting alleles from the current population – in other words, the chances of selecting a given allele is proportional to its frequency in the population as a whole.

At each generation, your program should calculate the frequency of all alleles and write them to a text file. At the end of the simulation, we'll be able to plot the frequencies on a chart to show the how they change over time.

---

1   Readers with a background in population genetics will, I hope, forgive the many shortcomings of this simulation!

Solution

This is a big exercise with a lot of parts, and there are many different ways to structure it. The solution we'll look at here is just one way; you may come up with something completely different.

The goal of this exercise is to write a program that combines object oriented and procedural code. We will start by tackling the object oriented part and defining some classes. We'll use three different classes – one to represent an individual, one to represent a locus, and one to represent an allele. Let's begin with the simplest class, the one that represents a single allele. It has a name, and a fitness score:

```
class Allele(object):
    def __init__(self, name, fitness):
        self.name = name
        self.fitness = fitness
```

A locus object is really only a way of grouping related alleles together, so all it needs is a name and a way of adding alleles. We could supply the list of alleles as part of the constructor, but just to make things easier to read we'll have the constructor create an empty list to hold the alleles, and write a method which allows us to add alleles one at a time:

```
class Locus(object):
    def __init__(self, name):
        self.name = name
        self.alleles = []

    def add_allele(self, allele):
        self.alleles.append(allele)
```

Finally, we need a class to represent an individual. An individual will have its list of alleles set when it's created, so we'll make the constructor take a list of alleles as its argument:

Chapter 4: object oriented Python

```
class Individual(object):

    def __init__(self, alleles):
        self.alleles = alleles
```

Having defined our classes, we can start experimenting with them. Let's start off with something simple – here's how we define a locus (which we'll imaginatively call **locus one**) with two alleles. As is customary, we'll use a capital letter **A** as the name for the most-fit allele (with a fitness of 1), and a lower-case **a** as the name for the less-fit allele (with a fitness slightly less than 1):

```
allele_A = Allele('A', 1)
allele_a = Allele('a', 0.94)
locus1 = Locus('locus one')
locus1.add_allele(allele_A)
locus1.add_allele(allele_a)
```

The first thing that we notice about this bit of code is that the variable names of the two alleles don't really serve any purpose – we create the `Allele` objects and then immediately add them to the `Locus` object. We can simplify the code a bit by calling the constructor for the alleles and then passing the returned value immediately to the `add_allele()` method all in one statement:

```
locus1 = Locus('locus one')
locus1.add_allele(Allele('A', 1))
locus1.add_allele(Allele('a', 0.94))
```

This has the exact same effect but is a little easier to read. Let's go ahead and create the other two loci in the same way, which we'll use for the rest of the exercise. We'll also create a list to hold all three `Locus` objects:

```
locus1 = Locus('locus one')
locus1.add_allele(Allele('A', 1))
locus1.add_allele(Allele('a', 0.94))

locus2 = Locus('locus two')
locus2.add_allele(Allele('B', 1))
locus2.add_allele(Allele('b', 0.76))

locus3 = Locus('locus three')
locus3.add_allele(Allele('C', 1))
locus3.add_allele(Allele('c', 0.81))

all_loci = [locus1, locus2, locus3]
```

Now we have our loci and alleles, we can create some individuals. Our `Individual` constructor requires that we pass in a list of alleles as the argument, so we need some way to get hold of the allele objects. Remember that we can't refer to the allele objects using their variable names, because we created them in such a way that they don't have variable names! Here's one way to do it – we could just grab the first element of the alleles list from each locus:

```
first_allele = locus1.alleles[0]
second_allele = locus2.alleles[0]
third_allele = locus3.alleles[0]
ind = Individual([first_allele, second_allele, third_allele])
```

or alternatively, using the list of loci:

```
alleles_for_individual = []
for locus in all_loci:
    alleles_for_individual.append(locus.alleles[0])
ind = Individual(alleles_for_individual)
```

This works fine, but if give all our one hundred individuals exactly the same set of alleles, then our simulation is going to be a bit boring! What we really need is a way of randomly picking an allele for each locus. A useful tool for this is the `random.choice()` method, which takes a list

Chapter 4: object oriented Python

of items as its argument and return a randomly selected element from that list. To use this method, we'll have to remember to import the `random` module.

This is where we start to see the difference between the procedural and object oriented way of thinking. We could easily write a function that takes a `Locus` as its argument and returns a random allele:

```
def get_random_allele(my_locus):
    return random.choice(my_locus.alleles)
```

But a more object oriented way of doing it is to add a method to the `Locus` class which returns a random allele:

```
class Locus(object):
    def __init__(self, name):
        ...

    def add_allele(self, allele):
        ...

    def get_random_allele(self):
        return random.choice(self.alleles)
```

Notice the difference between the two approaches: in the first approach, we get the information (the list of alleles) from the locus and then process it (pick a random allele) whereas in the second, we let the object use the information that it has (its list of alleles) to generate the answer for us. The distinction is subtle, but important.

Now we have a way of randomly picking alleles, we can write a function that creates and returns `Individuals` with randomly-picked alleles, given a set of loci:

```
def create_individual(loci):
    alleles_for_individual = []
    for locus in loci:
        alleles_for_individual.append(locus.get_random_allele())
    i = Individual(alleles_for_individual)
    return i
```

We can now create a starting population of any size we like just by calling this function inside a loop:

```
def create_population(size, loci):
    all_individuals = []
    for i in range(size):
        all_individuals.append(create_individual(loci))
    return all_individuals
my_population = create_population(100, all_loci)
```

Now we have a list containing one hundred `Individual` objects. Before we start tackling the selection/reproduction part of the simulation, it would be good to figure out a way to examine this population. We can think about examining the population in two different ways – we can ask questions about each `Individual` on its own, but we can also ask questions about the population as a whole.

Let's start by examining each individual on its own. For example, we might want to print the genotype (Abc, aBc, ABc, etc.) of each individual. Again, we're faced with the choice of whether to do this in a procedural or object oriented way. The procedural approach would be to write a function that takes an `Individual` object as its argument, and concatenates the name of each allele to generate the genotype:

```
def get_genotype_for_individual(ind):
    result = ''
    for allele in ind.alleles:
        result = result + allele.name
    return result
```

Chapter 4: object oriented Python

but the more object oriented approach is to add a `get_genotype()` method to the `Individual` class definition:

```
class Individual(object):

    def __init__(self, alleles):
        ...

    def get_genotype(self):
        result = ''
        for a in self.alleles:
            result = result + a.name
        return result
```

We can use this method to, for instance, print out the genotypes of each individual in the population in quite a natural way:

```
for ind in my_population:
    print(ind.get_genotype())
```

The output shows that this works just as we expect:

```
ABC
abC
aBc
aBC
AbC
abc
ABc
AbC
...etc...
```

Another obvious thing to do is to look at the fitness of each individual in the population. Again, there's a procedural and an object oriented way to do it – we'll implement the object oriented solution, which is to add a `get_fitness()` method to the `Individual` class definition:

```
class Individual(object):

    def __init__(self, alleles):
        ...

    def get_genotype(self):
        ...

    def get_fitness(self):
        final_fitness = 1
        for a in self.alleles:
            final_fitness = final_fitness * a.fitness
        return final_fitness
```

An individual can calculate its own fitness simply by multiplying up the fitnesses of each of its alleles. We can now look at both the genotype and fitness score for each individual:

```
for ind in my_population:
    print(ind.get_genotype(), ind.get_fitness())
```

The output looks good – we can see that, as expected, individuals with more capital letters in their genotype tend to have higher fitness than those with more lower case letters:

```
('Abc', 0.6156)
('aBc', 0.7614)
('ABC', 1)
('AbC', 0.76)
('aBc', 0.7614)
('aBC', 0.94)
('abc', 0.578664)
...
```

Now we've seen how to look at the data for individuals, let's tackle the problem of summarizing the population as a whole, starting with something easy – calculating the frequency of a given allele in the population. We simply iterate over the list of all individuals and ask, for

Chapter 4: object oriented Python

each individual, whether the given allele is in that individual's list of alleles:

```
def get_allele_frequency(population, allele):
    allele_count = 0
    for individual in population:
        if allele in individual.alleles:
            allele_count += 1
    return allele_count / len(population)
```

To use this function we first have to get a reference to one of our alleles. Remember that we don't have variables that point to the alleles, but we do have variables that point to the loci, so we can just grab the first allele in a loci's list of alleles and calculate its frequency:

```
# get the first allele for locus one
one_allele = locus1.alleles[0]
print(get_allele_frequency(my_population, one_allele))
```

The next logical step is to summarize a population by calculating the frequencies of all alleles. We can write a function that iterates over our list of loci and their alleles and prints the name and frequency of each one:

```
def summarize_population_alleles(population, loci):
    for locus in loci:
        for allele in locus.alleles:
            print(allele.name, get_allele_frequency(population, allele))

summarize_population_alleles(my_population, all_loci)
```

Th output shows pretty much what we'd expect – in the initial population, all alleles are hovering at a frequency of around 0.5, with some variation to due chance:

```
('A', 0.53)
('a', 0.47)
('B', 0.48)
('b', 0.52)
('C', 0.45)
('c', 0.55)
```

Now that we have a way to calculate the fitness of an individual, and a way to look at the allele frequencies in the population as a whole, we can make a start on the simulation aspect. Think about what has to happen in each generation: we need to look at each individual and figure out whether they die and get removed from the population. To figure out whether an individual dies, we just generate a random number between 0 and 1 (which we can do using the `random.random()` function) and if that number is greater than the individual's fitness, it gets removed from the population. Here's a bit of code that implements that idea:

```python
def single_generation(population):
    for individual in population:
        if random.random() > individual.get_fitness():
            population.remove(individual)
```

To test it out, we'll run the `single_generation()` function ten times on our initial population, printing the population size after each call. We'll print out the allele frequency summary at the start and end of the simulation so we can see what's happening. Here's the simulation code:

```python
summarize_population_alleles(my_population, all_loci)

for i in range(10):
    print('at generation ' + str(i))
    print('population size is ' + str(len(my_population)))
    single_generation(my_population)

summarize_population_alleles(my_population, all_loci)
```

simulation1.py

Chapter 4: object oriented Python

And the output shows what is happening. As the simulation progresses, the population size decreases (since we are removing individuals, but never adding them) and the frequency of the less fit alleles (the lower case ones) decreases while the frequency of the upper case ones increases[1]:

---

1 Remember that the make up of the starting population and the removal of individuals are both partly controlled by random numbers, so if you try running this code you'll get different results.

```
('A', 0.49)
('a', 0.51)
('B', 0.47)
('b', 0.53)
('C', 0.58)
('c', 0.42)
at generation 0
population size is 100
at generation 1
population size is 77
at generation 2
population size is 64
at generation 3
population size is 50
at generation 4
population size is 40
at generation 5
population size is 36
at generation 6
population size is 30
at generation 7
population size is 28
at generation 8
population size is 25
at generation 9
population size is 23
('A', 0.6086956521739131)
('a', 0.391304347826087)
('B', 0.8695652173913043)
('b', 0.13043478260869565)
('C', 0.9565217391304348)
('c', 0.043478260869565216)
```

Now all we need is to fill in the last bit of the simulation – adding new individuals to the population. As specified in the exercise description, we create a new individual by picking alleles randomly from the current population. There are a few different ways to do this, but the simplest one is probably to make a list, for each locus, of all the current alleles in the

Chapter 4: object oriented Python

population belonging to that locus, then pick a random element from that list:

```
def individual_from_population(population, loci):
    individual_alleles = []
    for locus in loci:
        # pick an allele from the population for this locus
        all_alleles = []
        for individual in population:
            for allele in individual.alleles:
                if allele in locus.alleles:
                    all_alleles.append(allele)

        # now all_alleles contains all the alleles in the population
        # for this locus, pick a random one
        this_allele = random.choice(all_alleles)
        individual_alleles.append(this_allele)

    # now individual_alleles contains all the alleles
    # for our new individual, one allele for each locus
    return Individual(individual_alleles)
```

All we have to do to complete our `single_generation()` function is to add enough new individuals to the population to make it back up to 100:

```
def single_generation(pop):
    for individual in pop:
        if random.random() > individual.get_fitness():
            pop.remove(individual)
    for i in range(100 - len(population)):
        pop.append(individual_from_population(population, all_loci))
```

simulation2.py

If we re-run our ten-generation simulation code from earlier, we can see that now the allele frequencies change, but the population size doesn't:

```
('A', 0.49)
('a', 0.51)
('B', 0.47)
('b', 0.53)
('C', 0.57)
('c', 0.43)
at generation 0
population size is 100
...
at generation 9
population size is 100
('A', 0.62)
('a', 0.38)
('B', 0.87)
('b', 0.13)
('C', 0.92)
('c', 0.08)
```

Having a snapshot of the allele frequencies at the start and end of the simulation is useful for testing, but it doesn't make for a very interesting result – what we would really like to be able to is look at the change in allele frequencies as the simulation progresses. To do that we'll have to switch from printing the frequency information on screen to writing it to a file. The simplest way to do this is just to write a line containing six comma-separated fields – one per allele – to a file after each generation. To make sense of the result, we'll need an extra bit of code to write a header line which will let us keep track of which field corresponds to which allele. Here's a function that will print a header line to an output file:

```
def summarize_alleles_header(loci, output_file):
    for locus in loci:
        for allele in locus.alleles:
            alleles_output.write(allele.name + ' , ')
    alleles_output.write('\n')
```

Chapter 4: object oriented Python

And here's a modified version of our earlier function that writes a single line summarizing the allele frequencies at a given moment:

```
def summarize_alleles(population, loci, output_file):
    for locus in loci:
        for allele in locus.alleles:
            freq = get_allele_frequency(population, allele)
            output_file.write(str(freq) + ', ')
    output_file.write('\n')
```

Now the main body of our simulation looks like this:

```
# create alleles and loci
locus1 = Locus('locus one')
locus1.add_allele(Allele('A', 1))
locus1.add_allele(Allele('a', 0.94))
locus2 = Locus('locus two')
locus2.add_allele(Allele('B', 1))
locus2.add_allele(Allele('b', 0.76))
locus3 = Locus('locus three')
locus3.add_allele(Allele('C', 1))
locus3.add_allele(Allele('c', 0.81))
all_loci = [locus1, locus2, locus3]

# create a population of 100 individuals
my_population = create_population(100, all_loci)

# open the alleles frequency output file and write the header line
alleles_output = open('alleles.csv', 'w')
summarize_alleles_header( all_loci, alleles_output)

# for each generation...
for i in range(10):
    # ...write a line of output to the file...
    summarize_alleles(my_population, all_loci, alleles_output)
    # ...then simulate death and reproduction
    single_generation(my_population)

# close the output file
alleles_output.close()
```

simulation2.py

And here's what the output file *alleles.csv* looks like – the first line tells us the order of the allele frequencies and subsequent lines each represent a single generation[1]:

```
A , a , B , b , C , c ,
0.54, 0.46, 0.41, 0.59, 0.4, 0.6,
0.52, 0.48, 0.49, 0.51, 0.46, 0.54,
0.6, 0.4, 0.59, 0.41, 0.48, 0.52,
0.62, 0.38, 0.67, 0.33, 0.46, 0.54,
0.64, 0.36, 0.73, 0.27, 0.47, 0.53,
0.65, 0.35, 0.83, 0.17, 0.47, 0.53,
0.66, 0.34, 0.83, 0.17, 0.53, 0.47,
0.7, 0.3, 0.81, 0.19, 0.58, 0.42,
0.72, 0.28, 0.88, 0.12, 0.62, 0.38,
0.74, 0.26, 0.92, 0.08, 0.66, 0.34,
```

We can trivially increase the number of generations in the simulation by changing the number in the `range()` function call. To visualize the results of our simulation, we can import the *alleles.csv* file into a spreadsheet package and draw some charts. Here's a chart showing allele frequencies over one hundred simulated generations:

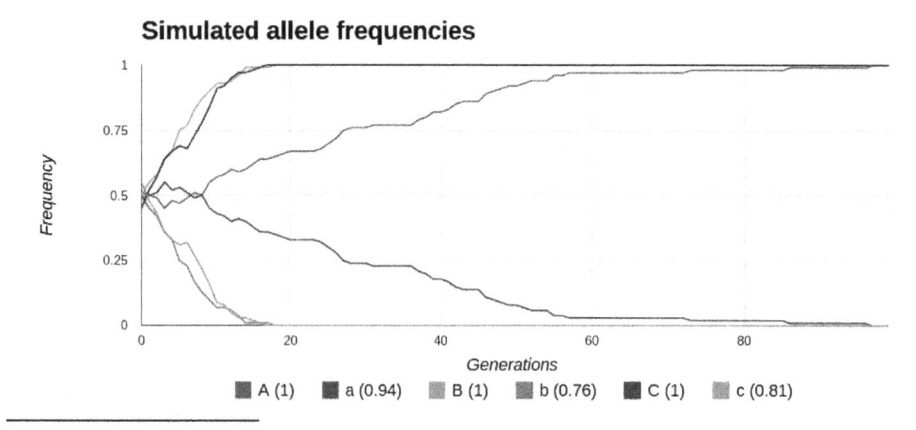

Simulated allele frequencies

Frequency vs *Generations*

■ A (1)   ■ a (0.94)   ■ B (1)   ■ b (0.76)   ■ C (1)   ■ c (0.81)

---

1   Ignore the trailing comma at the end of each line – we could remove it, but it would require more code and most spreadsheet programs will not care about it.

Chapter 4: object oriented Python

I've added the relative fitness for each allele (as set in the simulation code above) to the legend so we can see how the less-fit alleles with the lowest fitness (b and c) disappear from the population relatively early on, whereas the less-fit allele which has fairly high relative fitness (a) takes much longer to disappear (and even, due to chance, is more frequent than it's fitter partner A for a time).

5: Functional Python

Introduction

If you spend any time at all reading programming websites or blogs, then you can hardly have avoided discussions of *functional programming*. Although it's a very old idea, it's a hot topic right now[1] and much progress has been made recently in making it accessible to novice programmers. Functional programming is a tricky thing to define, however, and there are a few different ways to think about it. We'll start this chapter with a quick tour of important functional programming concepts.

State and mutability

One of the simplest ways to explain functional programming is to say that it's an approach to programming that tries as far as possible to avoid the use of *state*. By state, we simply mean variables that change during the execution of the program. Here's an example of a program with state – this program adds up the integers from zero to nine:

```
x = 0
for i in range(10):
    x = x + i
print(x)
```

We can tell that this program has state, because the value stored in the variable x changes as the program runs[2]. When the program starts, the value of x is 0. After the first iteration of the loop, the value of x is 1. After the second iteration, it's 3, and so on. Here's a program that does the same thing, without using state:

---

1   For reasons that we'll go into later.
2   Another way of saying this is to say that the variable x is *mutable*.

Chapter 5: Functional Python

```
x = sum(range(10))
print(x)
```

It works by using the built in `sum()` function, which takes as its argument a list[1] and returns the sum of all elements. Notice how, in this piece of code, the value of the variable x is set once, and then never changed (we'll see later in this chapter why this might be a desirable thing). From this perspective, functional programming appears to be the opposite of object oriented programming[2]. In object oriented programming, we create objects that have various attributes that describe their state (e.g. DNA sequences that have names and genetic codes) and we are mostly concerned with manipulating that state.

Side effects

Another way to think about functional programming is that it's a style of programming that avoids writing functions with side effects. A function is said to have side effects if, when you run it, it changes the state of the variables in the program. Here's an example of a function with side effects:

```
def my_function(i):
    i.extend(['a', 'b', 'c'])
    return(i)
```

This function takes a single argument, which is a list, and adds three more elements on to the end using the list `extend()` method before returning the extended list. The side effect, in this case, is that it changes the value of the list that's given as the argument. We can see this happen if we print the value of the list before and after running the function:

---

1 In fact, the argument can be anything that behaves like a list i.e. any iterable type.
2 If you haven't looked at the chapter on object oriented programming, now would be a good time to do so.

```
x = [1,2,3]
print(x)
print(my_function(x))
print(x)
```

```
[1, 2, 3]
[1, 2, 3, 'a', 'b', 'c']
[1, 2, 3, 'a', 'b', 'c']
```

After the function has run, the variable x contains three additional elements. Here's an example of a similar function that gives the same return value, but without the side effect – this function **doesn't** alter the value of the variable that's passed in as the argument:

```
def my_function(i):
    return(i + ['a', 'b', 'c'])
```

Why are side effects considered bad? The easiest answer is to pose the following question: imagine we have a variable x and we pass it as the argument to some function:

```
x = [1,4,9]
some_function(x)
// what is the value of x now?
```

If the function has side effects, then we have no way of knowing what the value of x is after the function call without going and looking at the code. Even worse, what we look inside the definition of `some_function()` and we find that it calls a bunch of other functions:

```
def some_function(input):
    some_other_function(input)
    another_function(input)
    yet_another_function(input)
```

Chapter 5: Functional Python

Now we have to go and look at the definitions of those functions in order to figure out whether they will change the value of x, and so on.

If, however, we know that `some_function()` doesn't have any side effects, then we can be confident that the value of x will not be changed by the function call, which makes it easier to reason about the behaviour of our program.

A closely related idea is the concept that a function should always return the same value if given the same input. If a function references variables other than its arguments, then it breaks this rule. For example, here's a function that takes as its argument a list, and appends the contents of the variable `to_add`:

```
def my_function(i):
    return(i + to_add)
```

It breaks the rule because the behaviour of the function changes depending on the value of `to_add` at the time that it's called. For example:

```
to_add =['a', 'b', 'c']
x = [1,2,3]
print(my_function(x))
to_add =['x', 'y', 'z']
print(my_function(x))
```

The two calls to `my_function` in the above code have exactly the same argument, but they return different results:

```
[1, 2, 3, 'a', 'b', 'c']
[1, 2, 3, 'x', 'y', 'z']
```

And of course, if we forget to define `to_add`, or it is not a list, then the function will generate an error.

Functions that satisfy the two criteria we have discussed above – they always return the same value when called with the same arguments, and they don't have any side effects – are called *pure functions*. For the reasons outlined above, it's generally much easier to reason about the behaviour of pure functions than functions that aren't pure.

Functions as objects

Yet another way of thinking about functional programming is the idea that functions are *objects* that can be passed around programs like any other type of object – they can be stored in variables, passed to other functions as arguments, and returned from other functions as return values. Python makes it quite easy to do this. By way of an example, here's a function that takes two arguments – a list and the name of a function – and prints out the result of running the function on each element of the list:

```
def print_list_with_function(my_list, my_function):
    for element in my_list:
        print(my_function(element))
```

list_function.py

This looks odd if you've not encountered it before, but the syntax should be familiar. The function iterates over the list, and for each element runs `my_function()` with the element as the input and passes the return value straight to the `print()` function. A function that takes another function as one of its arguments, as in the example above, is known as a *higher order function*.

Let's see what happens when we use it. Here, we create a list and pass it to our `print_list_with_function()` function, along with the name of the built in Python function `len()`, which returns the length of a string:

Chapter 5: Functional Python

```
input = ['abc', 'defhij', 'kl']
print_list_with_function(input, len)
```

As expected, the output contains the lengths of the three elements of our input list:

```
3
6
2
```

Here's where it gets interesting though; we're not restricted to using built in functions as the second argument to print_list_with_function(). We can supply any function we like as long as it takes a single string argument, including functions that we define. For example, here's a function that returns the second character of its argument:

```
def get_second(input):
    return input[1]
```

We can pass the name of this function (get_second()) as the last argument to print_list_with_function():

```
print_list_with_function(input, get_second)
```

And as expected, the output contains the second character of each element in our input list:

```
b
e
l
```

The get_second() function is a very short one – all it does is return a single expression. There's a special syntax for functions like these, called a *lambda expression*. It's like a compact version of a function definition, expect that the body of the function must be a single statement which is returned. Here's what the `get_second()` function looks like if we write it as a lambda expression:

```
get_second = lambda(input) : input[1]
```

You'll notice that it looks a bit different to a normal function definition. Rather than writing the name of the function followed by a list of its arguments in parentheses, instead we write the word *lambda* followed by the list of arguments. Also, we don't have to explicitly write the word *return* before the value that we want to return. Finally, it's all written on one line, and we store the result in a variable.

Once we've written our lambda expression and assigned the result to a variable, we can use it just like a normal function:

```
get_second = lambda(input) : input[1]
print_list_with_function(input, get_second)
```

We can also skip assigning the result of a lambda expression to a variable and use it directly. Here's the same code but with the result of the lambda expression passed directly to `print_list_with_function()`:

```
print_list_with_function(input, lambda(input) : input[1] )
```

A lambda expression that's used in this way is known as an *anonymous expression*[1], because it doesn't have a name. For very short functions, this alternative syntax is useful because it allows us to express code in a very concise way.

---

[1] Other programming languages have support for *anonymous functions*, which work the same way.

Chapter 5: Functional Python

What is to be calculated

The final way I want to suggest thinking about functional programming is that it places the emphasis on specifying **what the answer looks like**, rather than **how to calculate it**. Consider these two bits of code that add up the first ten integers and print out the result:

```
# procedural code
total = 0
for i in range(11):
    total = total + i
print(total)

# functional code
print(sum(range(11)))
```

In the first bit of code, we are giving the steps required to calculate the answer. If we were to translate this code into natural English, we might write:

> *Create a variable to hold a running total, and set it to zero. Then, for each number between zero and ten, add that number to the total. Finally, print the total.*

By contrast, in the second bit of code, we are simply describing the result:

> *The result is the sum of the numbers between zero and ten.*

and we are prepared to let the computer worry about how to actually calculate the answer. This idea is very similar to the different between iterative and recursive approaches to programming – take a look at the chapter on recursion if you haven't already done so.

The remainder of this chapter is divided into two main parts. In the first part, we will look at some built in higher order functions that allow us to carry out common programming tasks by using the techniques outlined above. In the second part, we'll see how we can use these same techniques in our own functions.

As you work through the rest of this chapter, bear in mind that, unlike in some other languages, functional programming in Python is not an all-or-nothing affair. It's not really feasible to write entire programs in a functional style[1], so when you use functional programming features in your programs they will generally be mixed in with procedural code.

built in higher order functions

There are many common programming tasks that can be made easier using higher order functions, and Python has very sensibly implemented several of them as built in functions. In this section we'll look at three higher order functions for working with iterable objects.

map

Consider the very common situation where you have a list of data, and you want to create a new list by carrying out some operation on each element of the old list. For example, you have a list of DNA sequences, and you want to create a list of their lengths. It's quite straightforward to do this with a `for` loop – we create en empty list to hold the result, then iterate over the input list adding a single element to the result on each iteration:

```
dna_list = ['TAGC', 'ACGTATGC', 'ATG', 'ACGGCTAG']
lengths = []
for dna in dna_list:
    lengths.append(len(dna))
# lengths is now [4,8,3,8]
```

---

[1] For one thing, a ban on side effects means that a purely functional program could never produce any output, since printing to the screen or to a file is a side effect!

Chapter 5: Functional Python

Here's a similar example – this time, we want to generate a list of the AT content of each sequence[1]:

```
dna_list = ['TAGC', 'ACGTATGC', 'ATG', 'ACGGCTAG']
at_contents = []
for dna in dna_list:
    at_contents.append((dna.count('A') + dna.count('T')) / len(dna))
```
map.py

These two examples share a lot of code between them. They both follow a general pattern – we start off by creating an empty list to hold the result, then we iterate over the list of DNA sequences, and for each sequence calculate some value and append it to the result list. The name for this general pattern, where we want to apply some function to each element of a list to generate a new list, is a *map*[2], and it's implemented in Python as a function called, unsurprisingly, `map()`.

To use the Python `map()` function, we have to supply a function that will take as its argument a single element of the input list and return the corresponding element in the output list (we'll call this the *transformation function*). For our first example – turning a list of DNA sequences into a list of their lengths – the built in `len()` function will do the job. For the second example – turning a list of DNA sequences into a list of their AT contents – we can write a simple function that returns the AT content of its argument:

```
from __future__ import division
def get_at(dna):
    return (dna.count('A') + dna.count('T')) / len(dna)
```

---

1 Remember to include `from __future__ import division` if you want to run this code in Python 2.
2 So-called because there's a one-to-one mapping between elements in the original list and the new list.

Now we simply have to call the `map()` function with the name of our transformation function as the first argument, and name of the original list as the second argument:

```
dna_list = ['TAGC', 'ACGTATGC', 'ATG', 'ACGGCTAG']
lengths = map(len, dna_list)
at_contents = map(get_at, dna_list)
```

map.py

The `map()` function takes care of setting up the empty results list, iterating over the original list, and running the transformation function on each element. The benefit of processing lists in this way is not simply that it involves less typing: rather, it's another way of achieving encapsulation. We have separated the bit of the code responsible for handling the iteration (the `map()` function) from the bit of code responsible for transforming a single element (the `get_at()` function).

Because the transformation functions that we pass to `map()` are often very short, it's quite common to use lambda expressions to do the job instead. Here's our AT content example written as a lambda expression. It's formatted over a few lines to make it easier to read:

```
at_contents = map(
    lambda dna : (dna.count('A') + dna.count('T')) / len(dna),
    dna_list
)
```

One final note about `map()`: its behaviour is subtly different in Python 2 and 3. In Python 2, the result of running a `map()` function is a straightforward list, but in Python 3, the result is a `map` object, which we can iterate over. This means that we can treat the returned value in pretty much the same way – this type of code will work fine in all versions of Python:

Chapter 5: Functional Python

```
dna_list = ['TAGC', 'ACGTATGC', 'ATG', 'ACGGCTAG']
at_contents = map(get_at, dna_list)
for at in at_contents:
    # do something with the AT content
```

but the way it works internally is slightly different. In Python 2, all elements of the resulting list are generated as soon as the `map()` function is called, but in Python 3, the elements are generated one-by-one as they are needed, a type of behaviour referred to as *lazy*. We can see the effects of this difference if we use `map()` to create a very large list. For example, here's a bit of code that first uses `range()` to create a list of the first hundred thousand integers, then uses `map()` to create a list of the first hundred thousand powers of two (i.e. the transformation function takes each element and calculates two to that power):

```
l = list(range(100000))
m = map(lambda x : 2 ** x, l)
```

Under Python 2, this statement will take a very long time to execute – around 30 seconds on my desktop computer[1]. However, under Python 3, the exact same statement executes in no time at all, because it doesn't start to actually calculate the elements until they are needed – for example, when we start to iterate over the `map` object:

```
l = list(range(100000))
m = map(lambda x : 2 ** x, l)
for i in m:
    print(i)
```

---

[1] See the section on performance in *Effective Python development for Biologists* for a detailed explanation of how to measure execution time.

```
0
1
4
9
16
25
36
49
64
81
...
```

Notice how this behaviour can catch us out if we try to use map() with a function that depends on side effects. Here's a bit of code where we define a transformation function that has the side-effect of appending the string 'a' to a list, x. We then call map() on a list of ten elements and print the value of x:

```
x = []
def square(input):
    x.append('a')
    return input ** 2

m = map(square, [0,1,2,3,4,5,6,7,8,9])
print(x)
```

Under Python 2, our square() function is run once for each element of our list when we call the map() function, so when we print x it contains ten elements:

```
['a', 'a', 'a', 'a', 'a', 'a', 'a', 'a', 'a', 'a']
```

But under Python 3, the square() function never runs, because we never access the elements of m, so the output shows us that even after the map() statement has completed, x is still an empty list:

Chapter 5: Functional Python

```
[]
```

This ability of Python 3 to carry out so-called *lazy evaluation*, which saves time and memory, is a nice illustration of the power of functional programming to simplify the process of reasoning about computation.

filter

A closely-related pattern to map is filter, used where we have a list from which we want to select only the elements that satisfy some condition. Imagine we have a list of DNA sequences, and we want to create a new list containing only the sequences longer than five bases. The iterative solution is quite straightforward:

```
dna_list = ['TAGC', 'ACGTATGC', 'ATG', 'ACGGCTAG']
long_dna = []
for dna in dna_list:
    if len(dna) > 5:
        long_dna.append(dna)
```

filter.py

But if we look at another example – creating a new list that contains only the sequences whose AT content is less than 0.6 – we can see how repetitive this kind of code is:

```
from __future__ import division
dna_list = ['TAGC', 'ACGTATGC', 'ATG', 'ACGGCTAG']

at_poor_dna = []
for dna in dna_list:
    print(dna, get_at(dna))
    if (dna.count('A') + dna.count('T')) / len(dna) < 0.6:
        at_poor_dna.append(dna)
```

Chapter 5: Functional Python

Just as with map, Python has a built in function for doing this kind of filtering, and it works in a similar way. We supply the Python's filter function with the name of a function that takes a single element as its argument and returns True or False to indicate whether or not that element should be included in the result list. Here's how we use it to select only DNA sequences longer than five bases[1]:

```
dna_list = ['TAGC', 'ACGTATGC', 'ATG', 'ACGGCTAG']

def is_long(dna):
    return len(dna) > 5

long_dna = filter(is_long, dna_list)
```

filter.py

And here's how we use it to select only DNA sequence whose AT content is less than 0.6:

```
from __future__ import division
dna_list = ['TAGC', 'ACGTATGC', 'ATG', 'ACGGCTAG']

def is_at_poor(dna):
    at = (dna.count('A') + dna.count('T')) / len(dna)
    return at < 0.6

at_poor_dna = filter(is_at_poor, dna_list)
```

Just as with map(), filter() behaves differently under Python 2 and 3, returning a list and a filter object respectively. So just as with map(), it's important not to rely on any side effects in the function that we pass to filter().

---

1   Both of the examples here could be re-written as lambda expressions.

Chapter 5: Functional Python

sorted

You've probably already encountered the `sorted()` function and used it for sorting lists in alphabetical or numerical order. The `sorted()` function is actually capable of sorting elements using any type of custom ordering, and it does so by acting as a higher order function. Sorting is a little bit more complicated to understand than mapping or filtering: the sorting algorithm used by Python is quite complicated so, unlike `map()` and `filter()`, we can't show a simple imperative version of the code. Nevertheless, the same principle of encapsulation applies: just as with `map()` (where we we supply a function that tells Python how to transform a single input element and Python takes care of producing the output list) and `filter()` (where we supply a function that tells Python whether to include a single input element and Python takes care of producing the filtered list), with `sorted()` we supply a function that tells Python what **property** of each input element we want to sort on, and Python takes care of producing the sorted list.

A few examples will make this clearer. Let's start by sorting our list of DNA sequences using the default order (i.e. without supplying a custom function):

```
dna_list = ['TAGC', 'ACGTATGC', 'ATG', 'ACGGCTAG']
sorted_dna = sorted(dna_list)
print(sorted_dna)
print(dna_list)
```
sorted.py

As the output makes clear, this gives us an alphabetical sorting of the elements in the list:

```
['ACGGCTAG', 'ACGTATGC', 'ATG', 'TAGC']
['TAGC', 'ACGTATGC', 'ATG', 'ACGGCTAG']
```

It's very important to note that, as we can see from the second line of output, the original list is unchanged. There is another way of sorting a list – we can call the `sort()` method on the list – but we're going to avoid using that method in this section for two reason. First, using `sorted()` to create a sorted copy of the list is more compatible with the functional programming ideas of avoiding state and mutability. Second, the `sorted()` method is more flexible as it's not restricted to lists – we can call sorted on any iterable data type (strings, files, etc).

Now let's look at sorting in a different order – for example, by length. To do this, we supply `sorted()` with a *key function*. The key function must take a single argument, and return the value that we want to sort on. By convention, we supply the key function as a keyword argument like this:

```
sorted(some_list, key=my_key_function)
```

For sorting by length, we can use the built in `len()` function as our key function. The `len()` function takes a single argument, and returns a single value, so it satisfies the requirements for a key function and we can use it like this:

```
dna_list = ['TAGC', 'ACGTATGC', 'ATG', 'ACGGCTAG']
sorted_dna = sorted(dna_list, key=len)
print(sorted_dna)
```

sorted.py

This gives us our DNA sequences sorted from shortest to longest:

```
['ATG', 'TAGC', 'ACGTATGC', 'ACGGCTAG']
```

If we want them in the reverse order then we can simply pass a `reverse` keyword argument to the `sorted` function:

Chapter 5: Functional Python

```
sorted_dna = sorted(dna_list, key=len, reverse=True)
```

Let's look at something a bit more complicated that requires a custom key function: sorting by AT content. We already have a function that takes a single DNA sequence and returns the AT content from our `map()` example above, so we can just reuse it for `sorted()`:

```
from __future__ import division
def get_at(dna):
    return (dna.count('A') + dna.count('T')) / len(dna)

dna_list = ['TAGC', 'ACGTATGC', 'ATG', 'ACGGCTAG']
sorted_dna = sorted(dna_list, key=get_at)
print(sorted_dna)
```

As the output shows, we get the DNA sequences sorted from lowest AT content to highest:

```
['ACGGCTAG', 'TAGC', 'ACGTATGC', 'ATG']
```

Here's another example – imagine that we want to sort a set of DNA sequences by the length of their poly-A tail. We need a function takes a DNA sequence as its argument, and return the number of A bases at the end of the sequence. One way to write such a function is using a regular expression. In the function below we check for the existence of a poly-A pattern at the end of the input sequence, and return either the length of the match (if one is found) or zero (if there is no match):

```
import re
def poly_a_length(dna):
    poly_a_match = re.search(r'A+$', dna)
    if poly_a_match:
        return len(poly_a_match.group())
    else:
        return 0
```

Having written this function, we can use it as the key argument in a `sorted()` function call to sort a list of DNA sequences by the length of their poly-A tails:

```
dna_list = ['ATCGA', 'ACGG', 'CGTAAA', 'ATCGAA']
print(sorted(dna_list, key=poly_a_length))
```

```
['ACGG', 'ATCGA', 'ATCGAA', 'CGTAAA']
```

All of the above examples involve sorting strings, but we can use sorted to sort any type of data. Imagine we have a list of tuples, each of which contains the name of a gene, and an expression level measurement under two different conditions:

```
measurements = [
    ('gene1', 121, 98),
    ('gene2', 56,  32),
    ('gene3', 1036, 1966),
    ('gene4', 543, 522)
]
```

sort_tuples.py

Our aim is to identify genes which are over-expressed in the second condition relative to the first: in other words, we want to sort the tuples by the ratio of the two measurements. Our key function, therefore, must take a single tuple as its argument, and return the result of dividing the third element by the second[1] to get the ratio:

```
from __future__ import division
def get_ratio(measurement):
    return measurement[2] / measurement[1]
```

---

1   Remember that these will be at index 2 and 1 respectively.

Chapter 5: Functional Python

Since we are interested in the genes for which the ratio is highest, we should probably pass the `reverse=True` parameter to `sorted()`, so that the genes with the highest ratio (i.e. the most over-expression in condition two) appear at the top of the list:

```
print(sorted(measurements, key=get_ratio, reverse=True))
```

```
[('gene3', 1036, 1966), ('gene4', 543, 522), ('gene1', 121, 98), ('gene2', 56, 32)]
```

The sorting algorithm used by Python[1] is *stable*, meaning that elements which are equal (more accurately: which are equal after being run through the key function) are kept in the same order. This is a very useful property, as it allows us to carry out complex sorts by combining a number of simple sorts. Imagine we have a list of tuples representing loci, each of which has a chromosome number, a base number, and a locus name:

```
loci = [
    (4, 9200, 'gene1'),
    (6, 63788, 'gene2'),
    (4, 7633, 'gene3'),
    (2, 8766, 'gene4')
]
```

sort_chromosomes.py

We want to sort the loci by chromosome number and then, within each chromosome, by base position. We start off by defining functions which will return, for a given locus, either the chromosome number or the base (simply by returning the first or second element of the tuple):

---

1   Timsort, if you're interested: http://en.wikipedia.org/wiki/Timsort

```
def get_chromosome(locus):
    return locus[0]

def get_base_position(locus):
    return locus[1]
```

We now carry out two sorts – first by base, then by chromosome:

```
sorted_by_base = sorted(loci, key=get_base_position)
final_sort = sorted(sorted_by_base, key=get_chromosome)
print(final_sort)
```

to get the result we want:

```
[(2, 8766, 'gene4'), (4, 7633, 'gene3'), (4, 9200, 'gene1'), (6, 63788, 'gene2')]
```

reduce

The final higher order function that we'll look at is `reduce()` – probably the least commonly-used of Python's built in higher order functions. Just like the other higher order functions we've looked at, `reduce()` takes two arguments – a function, and a list. It then starts using the function to reduce the list to a single value (hence its name). First it calls the function with the first two elements of the list as arguments and stores the result. Then it repeatedly calls the function using the result of the last call and the next element in the list as arguments, repeating this until it runs out of elements in the list, at which point the result is returned. We can see from this description of `reduce()` that it differs from the other higher order functions in two important ways: the function that we pass in as the first argument must take two arguments and return a single value, and the overall result of calling `reduce()` will be a single value rather than a list.

Chapter 5: Functional Python

An example will make it clearer: say we wanted to find the product of a list of numbers. We can write a function that takes two arguments and multiplies them together:

```python
def multiply(x,y):
    return x * y
```

We can then take this function and pass it to `reduce()` along with our list of numbers:

```python
numbers = [2,6,3,8,5,4]
print(reduce(multiply, numbers))
```

reduce.py

and follow what happens. First, `reduce()` will call `multiply()` using the first two elements of the list – 2 and 6 – as arguments and get the result 12. It will then call `multiply()` using the third element of the list (3) and the result of the last call (12) as arguments and get the result 36. It will then call `multiply()` using the fourth element of the list (8) and the result of the last call (36) as arguments, and so on, until all elements have been multiplied and it returns the final answer, 5760.

Real life examples of situations where reduce is useful are hard to come by, but we have already encountered an example in this book. Recall that in the chapter on recursion, our solution to the last common ancestor exercise involved the same strategy as `reduce()`. To find the last common ancestor of a list of nodes in a tree given a function that can find the last common ancestor of any two nodes, we first found the last common ancestor of the first two nodes, then found the last common ancestor of that result and the third node, and so on. We can concisely express this strategy using `reduce()`:

```
def find_lca_of_two(node1, node2):
    ...

def find_lca_of_list(node_list):
    return(reduce(find_lca_of_two, node_list))
```

Writing higher order functions

We'll round up this chapter with a look at how we can take advantage of the functional features of Python to write our own higher order functions. Opportunities to employ functional features can be hard to spot when you're not used to them, so let's start by asking the following question: when would we benefit from writing a higher order function? Just like a normal function, a higher order function lets us abstract part of the behaviour of a bit of code to make it more flexible. Here's an example: imagine we're writing a program that, at some point, needs to generate a list of overlapping 4mers for a DNA sequence, so we write a function that looks like this:

```
def get_4mers(dna):
    4mers = []
    for i in range(len(dna) - 3):
        4mers.append(dna[i:i+4])
    return 4mers
```

Later, we're working on another program that needs to generate a list of overlapping 6mers, so we write another bit of code:

```
def get_6mers(dna):
    6mers = []
    for i in range(len(dna) - 5):
        6mers.append(dna[i:i+6])
    return 6mers
```

Chapter 5: Functional Python

It's very obvious, looking at the two functions, that they are doing the same thing with one small difference: the length of the kmers that they are generating. So we abstract that part of the function's behaviour by turning it into an argument:

```
def get_kmers(dna, k):
    kmers = []
    for i in range(len(dna) - k +1):
        kmers.append(dna[i:i+k])
    return kmers
```

By turning that particular aspect of the function's behaviour – the kmer size – into an argument, we have created a more flexible function that can generate kmers of any length.

Now let's imagine that we want a function that returns not the kmers themselves, but the AT content of the kmers (perhaps we are using the kmers to survey the variation in AT content along a chromosome using a sliding window approach). We can take our `get_kmers()` function and modify it accordingly:

```
from __future__ import division
def get_kmers_at(dna, k):
    result = []
    for i in range(len(dna) - k +1):
        kmer = dna[i:i+k]
        at = (kmer.count('A') + kmer.count('T')) / k
        result.append(at)
    return result
```

Next, we want a function that returns the number of CG dinucleotides in each kmer (perhaps we are looking for regions of a chromosome subject to CpG methylation). We can do this with yet another modification of `get_kmers()`:

```
def get_kmers_cg(dna, k):
    result = []
    for i in range(len(dna) - k +1):
        kmer = dna[i:i+k]
        cg = kmer.count('CG')
        result.append(cg)
    return result
```

Now we find ourselves in the same situation as before – we have two very similar functions, and we want to combine them to make a single, flexible function. But what is it that needs to be abstracted in this case? In other words, what is it that differs between the two functions? It's not a simple variable, but rather **the process that is applied to each kmer to generate a single element of the result list**. So to make our flexible, generic function, we take this process – let's call it the analyze kmer function – and turn it into an argument:

```
def get_kmers_f(dna, k, analyze_kmer):
    result = []
    for i in range(len(dna) - k +1):
        kmer = dna[i:i+k]
        result.append(analyze_kmer(kmer))
    return result
```

analyze_kmers.py

The above version of the function takes three arguments – the DNA sequence, the kmer length, and the name of the function which analyses a kmer – and returns a list containing the result of running the analyze_kmer() function on each kmer generated from the input sequence. Just like with map(), filter() and sorted(), the analyze_kmer() function has to follow a specific set of rules. It must take as its argument a DNA string, and it must return a single value. Our get_at() function from earlier in the chapter follows these rules, therefore we can pass it as the third argument to get_kmers_f(). In

Chapter 5: Functional Python

fact, doing so reproduces the functionality of the get_kmers_at() function we looked at earlier:

```
dna = 'ATCGATCATCGGCATCGATCGGTATCAGTACGTAC'
at_scores = get_kmers_f(dna, 8, get_at)
```

And we can reproduce the functionality of get_kmers_cg() using either another function or simply a lambda expression:

```
dna = 'ATCGATCATCGGCATCGATCGGTATCAGTACGTAC'
cg_counts = get_kmers_f(dna, 8, lambda dna : dna.count('CG'))
```

What have we actually achieved by structuring our code in this way? It all comes back to the idea of encapsulation: separating out code that does different jobs. Rather than having a function that does two jobs as in the case of get_kmers_at() (generating kmers and calculating AT scores), we now have one function whose job is to generate kmers, and a separate function whose job is to calculate AT scores. We can use these single-purpose functions as building blocks to easily make more complex pieces of code. In fact, what we have really built here in the form of the get_kmers_f function is a specialized kind of map function – one designed to work on DNA sequences.

There's one other aspect to higher order functions that you're less likely to encounter: we can write a function that returns another function – a kind of *function factory*. Here's an example: imagine we want to write a function that will take a DNA sequence as its argument, identify cut sites for the EcoRI restriction enzyme (which cuts at the pattern GAATTC), and return a list of the DNA fragments that would be produced by an EcoRI digest of the input sequence. The function is quite easy to write using Python's regular expression module[1] – we just have to be careful to add an

---

[1] We don't actually need a regular expression, as the EcoRI cut site motif has no variation, but the re.finditer function is a useful way to iterate over pattern matches.

Chapter 5: Functional Python

offset of one to the match position to allow for the fact that EcoRI cuts after the first base, and not forget to include the final fragment in the return list:

```
def ecori_digest(dna):
    current_position = 0
    result = []
    for m in re.finditer('GAATTC', dna):
        result.append(dna[current_position:m.start() + 1])
        current_position = m.start() + 1
    result.append(dna[current_position:])
    return result
```

Next, we realize that this function would be more useful if it could generate fragments for any given restriction enzyme motif (with the accompanying offset). Normally, we'd do this by modifying the `digest` function to take a pattern and offset as additional arguments[2], but here's a different approach – we can instead write a function that takes a pattern and offset as arguments, and returns a new function that will carry out the digest:

```
def make_digester(pattern, offset):

    def digester(dna):
        current_position = 0
        result = []
        for m in re.finditer(pattern, dna):
            result.append(dna[current_position:m.start() + offset])
            current_position = m.start() + offset
        result.append(dna[current_position:])
        return result

    return digester  ❶
```

digester.py

---

2   See the regular expression chapter of *Python for Biologists* for a discussion of this.

Notice what's going on here: the `digester()` function is being defined **inside** the `make_digester()` function, using the variables that were passed to the `make_digester()` function. The newly created `digester()` function is returned from inside `make_digester()` ❶. To use the `make_digester()` function, we call it with a pattern and an offset and store the returned value as a variable:

```
ecori_digester = make_digester('GAATTC', 1)
print(ecori_digester(dna))
```

In the code above, the variable `ecori_digester` points to the function that was created by `make_digester()`. No calculations are actually carried out until the second statement, where the `ecori_digester()` function is called. We can use the `make_digester()` function factory to make multiple different functions that will generate fragments for different restriction enzymes:

```
ecori_digester = make_digester('GAATTC', 1)
print(ecori_digester(dna))

ecorv_digester = make_digester('GATATC', 3)
print(ecorv_digester(dna))
```

```
['CGATG', 'AATTCTATCGATATCGTGA']
['CGATGAATTCTATCGAT', 'ATCGTGA']
```

Notice how when we call the newly created functions, we don't have to pass in the pattern and offset as arguments, since these are effectively already part of the function definition.

It's rare to see this technique in real world code, since the situations in which it is useful are often better handled using normal functions. Even the example above could be implemented more easily using *partial function application*, a functional programming technique whereby a function has some of its argument fixed (here, `pattern` and `offset`) to yield another function with a smaller number of arguments.

Recap

We started this chapter with a brief overview of a few different ways of looking at functional programming. The concepts introduced here – like immutability and side effects – are useful to know about, even if you don't follow a particularly functional style of programming. We also covered a feature of the Python language that makes function programming possible: the ability to manipulate functions like any other data type.

We then took a quick look at three built in Python list manipulation functions that exploit Python functional features: `map()`, `filter()` and `sorted()`. All three take functions as arguments, making them higher order functions, and all three are highly flexible as a result.

Finally, we saw how we can use those same functional features to write higher order functions of our own. As with so many programming techniques, the value of higher order functions lies in their ability to encapsulate code and allow for separation of concerns.

Chapter 5: Functional Python

Exercises

BLAST processor

The file *blast_result.txt* in the *functional_python* folder of the exercises download contains a BLAST result in tabular format. Each row represents a hit and the fields, in order, give:

1. the name of the query sequence
2. the name of the subject sequence
3. the percentage of positions that are identical between the two sequences
4. the alignment length
5. the number of mismatches
6. the number of gap opens
7. the position of the start of the match on the query sequence
8. the position of the end of the match on the query sequence
9. the position of the start of the match on the subject sequence
10. the position of the end of the match on the subject sequence
11. the evalue for the hit
12. the bit score for the hit

Use a combination of `map`, `filter` and `sorted` to answer the following questions:

- How many hits have fewer than 20 mismatches?

- List the subject sequence names for the ten matches with the lowest percentage of identical positions
- For matches where the subject sequence name includes the string "COX1", list the start position on the query as a proportion of the length of the match

FASTA processor

Write a function that copies FASTA format sequences from an input file to an output file while allowing for arbitrary modification of both the header and the sequence. Your function should take four arguments: the name of the input file, the name of the output file, a header-modification function and a sequence-modification function.

Write some code that uses your FASTA copying function to fix these common FASTA file problems, one at a time:

- The sequence is in lower case and you need it in upper case
- The sequence contains unknown bases that should be removed
- The headers contain spaces that should be changed to underscores
- The headers are too long and need to be truncated to ten characters

Write some code that uses your FASTA copying function to modify the header for each sequence. Try the following, one at a time:

- Append the length of the sequence to the header
- Append the AT content of the sequence to the header
- If the sequence starts with ATG and ends with a poly-A tail, append the phrase "putative transcript" to the header

Chapter 5: Functional Python

Use the file *sequences.fasta* in the *functional_programming* folder of the exercises download to test your code.

Solutions

BLAST processor

We can make a fair bit of progress on this problem just by thinking about the overall strategy for solving it. We know that `map()`, `filter()` and `sorted()` work on lists, so we know that we're going to have to read in our BLAST result file and turn it into a list, where each element represents a single hit.

But how should we store each individual element – should it be a string, a tuple, a dict, an object? All of these approaches will work, but for now let's just take the simplest possible approach and store each hit as a string read directly from the file. We can do this by creating an empty list, opening the file, reading each line, and appending it to the list:

```
lines = []
for line in open('blast_result.txt'):
    lines.append(line)
```

But wait: `map()`, `filter()` and `sorted()` don't **just** work on lists, they work on **any** iterable type (i.e. any type of data that we can use in a loop). We know that file objects are iterable, so we don't have to bother creating a list – we can just ask `map()`, `filter()` or `sorted()` to process a file object directly, and it will "see" the individual lines. In other words, we can just write something like:

```
f = open('some_file.txt')
g = filter(some_function, f)
```

And `filter()` will process each line of the file in turn.

Chapter 5: Functional Python

With that in mind, we can start working on a filter function to answer the first question – how many hits have fewer than 20 mismatches. This seems straightforward: we know that the fields in each line are separated by tab characters, and that the number of mismatches is the fifth field, so all we have to do in our filter function is split the line using tabs, take the fifth element of the resulting list, and ask if it's less than 20:

```
def mismatch_filter(hit_string):
    mismatch_count = hit_string.split("\t")[4]
    return mismatch_count < 20

lines = filter(mismatch_filter, open('blast_result.txt'))
```

Unfortunately, running this code causes an error:

```
IndexError: list index out of range
```

and if we take another look at the input file, we can see why:

```
# BLASTX 2.2.27+
# Query: gi|322830704:1426-2962 Boreus elegans mitochondrion...
# Database: nem.fasta
# Fields: query id, subject id, % identity, ...
# 405 hits found
gi|322830704:1426-2962  gi|225622197|ref|YP...
```

The first five lines are comments, which give information on the version of BLAST which generated the file, the name of the database, etc. Because these lines don't follow the tab-separated standard expected by the `mismatch_filter()` function, splitting them on tabs returns a list with fewer than five elements.

To remove these comment lines, we could add an extra check to our `mismatch_filter()` function:

```
def mismatch_filter(hit_string):
    if line.startswith('#'):
        return False
    mismatch_count = hit_string.split("\t")[4]
    return mismatch_count < 20
```

but, thinking ahead, these lines are going to be a problem for all parts of this exercise, so why not create a filter function just to remove them? This way, we'll be able to reuse it for the other parts of the exercise:

```
def comment_filter(line):
    return not line.startswith('#')

hit_lines = filter(comment_filter, open('blast_result.txt'))
```

Now we can simply run our existing `mismatch_filter()` on the non-comment lines and ask for the length of the filtered list[1]:

```
f = filter(mismatch_filter, hit_lines)
print(len(f))
```

Unfortunately, this bit of code prints zero[2] – clearly not the correct result. The problem is that in the `mismatch_filter()` function we're comparing the fifth field of the input file (which is a string) with the value 20 (which is an integer). Since, under the rules of Python, any string is always "bigger" than any integer, the function always returns `False`. We can fix the problem by turning the `mismatch_count` variable into an integer:

---

1   Remember that in Python 3, the result of filter is not a list but a filter object, so to get this bit of code to run under Python 3 we need to convert the filter object to a list before asking for the length: `print(len(list(f)))`
2   Unless you're using Python 3, in which case it will case a TypeError

Chapter 5: Functional Python

```
def mismatch_filter(hit_string):
    mismatch_count = int(hit_string.split("\t")[4])
    return mismatch_count < 20
```
blast_filter.py

And now we get the correct answer of 25.

On to the next section of the exercise: listing the subject sequence names for the ten matches with the lowest percentage of identical positions. This is going to be a three-step process: we need to sort the lines by the percent identity field, take the first ten lines of the resulting list, and then extract the subject sequence names from those lines.

To sort by percent identity, we need a key function that extracts the percent identity from a hit – in other words, a function that takes the entire hit string as its argument and return just the percent identity. Having learned the lesson about string/numerical data types in the previous bit of the exercise, we will be sure to convert the percent identity to a number – in this case a floating point number, rather than an integer – before returning it:

```
def get_percent_id(hit_string):
    return float(hit_string.split("\t")[2])

s = sorted(hit_lines, key=get_percent_id)
```

The next step is to take the first ten elements of the sorted list and assign them to a variable:

```
low_id_hits = s[0:10]
```

Remember that the individual elements of `low_id_hits` are complete hit strings, not percentage identity scores – `sorted()` doesn't change the elements of the input list, it just re-orders them.

Finally, we need to turn each complete hit string into a subject sequence name using a mapping function. The code for the mapping function is very similar to the code for our filtering function: in both cases, we are simply taking a string, splitting it, and returning one of the resulting elements (in this case, the second element):

```
def get_subject(hit_string):
    return hit_string.split("\t")[1]
```

All we have to do to get the answer we want is to use `map()` to process the low id hits using the `get_subject()` function, and print out the results one by one. Here's the whole program:

```
def comment_filter(line):
    return not line.startswith('#')

def get_percent_id(hit_string):
    return float(hit_string.split("\t")[2])

def get_query(hit_string):
    return hit_string.split("\t")[1]

hit_lines = filter(comment_filter, open('blast_result.txt'))
f = filter(mismatch_filter, hit_lines)
s = sorted(hit_lines, key=get_percent_id)
low_id_hits = s[0:10]
for subject in map(get_query, low_id_hits):
    print(subject)
```

blast_filter.py

and here's the output:

Chapter 5: Functional Python

```
gi|336287915|gb|AEI30246.1|
gi|336287919|gb|AEI30248.1|
gi|336287881|gb|AEI30229.1|
gi|336287897|gb|AEI30237.1|
gi|336287895|gb|AEI30236.1|
gi|336287917|gb|AEI30247.1|
gi|336287921|gb|AEI30249.1|
gi|336287923|gb|AEI30250.1|
gi|336287885|gb|AEI30231.1|
gi|336287889|gb|AEI30233.1|
```

Now for the last bit of the exercise – for matches where the subject sequence name includes the string "COX1", list the start position on the query as a proportion of the length of the match. This obviously involves a filter for the first part (selecting only hits with "COX1" in the subject name) and, though it may not be obvious at first, we can use map() to address the second part.

First the filter, and most of this code looks quite familiar by now. We split the input line using tabs, get the element we're looking for, and return True or False depending on whether or not the element contains the string "COX1":

```
def cox1_filter(hit_string):
    subject = hit_string.split("\t")[1]
    if "COX1" in subject:
        return True
    else:
        return False
```

Now the map. For this function, we need to extract two bits of information from the hit line – the query start and the length – then divide one by the other and return the result:

```
from __future__ import division

def start_ratio(hit_string):
    query_start = int(hit_string.split("\t")[6])
    hit_length = int(hit_string.split("\t")[3])
    return query_start / hit_length
```

Having written our two functions, getting the answer is just a case of applying them in the right order (not forgetting to filter out the comment lines):

```
def comment_filter(line):
    return not line.startswith('#')

def cox1_filter(hit_string):
    subject = hit_string.split("\t")[1]
    if "COX1" in subject:
        return True
    else:
        return False

def start_ratio(hit_string):
    query_start = int(hit_string.split("\t")[6])
    hit_length = int(hit_string.split("\t")[3])
    return query_start / hit_length


hit_lines = filter(comment_filter, open('blast_result.txt'))
f = filter(cox1_filter, hit_lines)
for ratio in map(start_ratio, f):
    print(ratio)
```

blast_filter.py

Chapter 5: Functional Python

```
0.0226244343891
0.00900900900901
0.0226244343891
0.0226244343891
0.0226244343891
0.0226244343891
0.00779727095517
0.0430839002268
```

FASTA processor

This exercise is an example of a task that crops up pretty regularly in bioinformatics work flows. We want to parse some complex file format, tinker with a specific bit of data, then put it all back together again in the same format.

Let's start off by writing a function that does nothing but read records from a FASTA file, split them into header and sequence, then write the header and sequence out to another file. This function won't do anything useful, but it will provide a nice framework for solving the rest of the exercise. To keep things simple, we'll assume that the sequence for each FASTA record is on a single line – i.e. the FASTA file looks like this:

```
>sequence1
actgatcgatcgatcgatcaatcgatcgacgatcgattacgtacgatcgtacgtacgtc
>sequence2
ttagcagtgactgtactctgtactacgtgctagtagctgtagctagtacc
```

and not like this:

```
>sequence1
actgatcgatcgatcg
atcaatcgatcgacga
tcgattacgtacgatc
gtacgtacgtc
>sequence2
ttagcagtgactgtac
tctgtactacgtgcta
gtagctgtagctagta
cc
```

which would make the parsing code more complex.

Here's the straightforward copying function:

Chapter 5: Functional Python

```
def fasta_copy(source, destination):
    output = open(destination, "w")
    header = ""
    for line in open(source):
        if line.startswith('>'):
            header = line.rstrip("\n")[1:]
        else:
            sequence = line.rstrip("\n")
            output.write('>' + header +"\n")
            output.write(sequence + "\n")
```

There's not too much going on here. We just iterate over the input file line by line, checking to see if it starts with a greater-than symbol. If it does, then it's a header line, in which case we set the value of the header variable to be the contents of the line starting at the second character (i.e. we remove the greater-than symbol). If it doesn't, then it's a sequence line, in which case we write out the header and the sequence in FASTA format to the output file (remembering to put the greater-than symbol back on the start of the header).

The next step is to turn our `fasta_copy()` function into a true higher order function by allowing it to modify the header and sequence before they're written to the output file. Doing this requires surprisingly little change in the code – we just have to add a `process_header()` function and a `process_sequence()` function as arguments, and to run the header and sequence through the appropriate functions before writing them to the output:

```
def fasta_copy(source, destination, process_header, process_sequence):
    output = open(destination, "w")
    header = ""
    for line in open(source):
        if line.startswith('>'):
            header = process_header(line.rstrip("\n")[1:])
        else:
            sequence = process_sequence(line.rstrip("\n"))
            output.write('>' + header +"\n")
            output.write(sequence + "\n")
```

Attempting to use this code to solve the first bit of the exercise – change the sequence from lower case to upper case – we run into a problem. The `fasta_copy()` function demands that we supply a function to process the header, but for this particular job, we don't want to change the header. We can't simply call `fasta_copy()` with only three arguments (`source`, `destination`, and a `process_sequence` function) because that will cause an error – it requires four. The solution is to define a "do-nothing" function that simply returns its input[1]:

```
def do_nothing(x):
    return x
```

Now we can define a function that converts its input to upper case:

```
def to_upper(dna):
    return dna.upper()
```

and make the call to our `fasta_copy()` function:

```
fasta_copy('sequences.fasta', 'corrected.fasta', do_nothing, to_upper)
```

Sure enough, when we open up the file *corrected.fasta* in a text editor, we can see that the sequence which was in lower case in *sequences.fasta* has been converted to upper case:

---

1 This is technically known as an identity function, and some languages (though not Python) have one as part of their standard library.

Chapter 5: Functional Python

```
>sequence_in_lowercase
ACTGATCATCATCACTCGATCGACTACTATCGATGTCGATCTCATCGTAG
```

On to the next bit of the exercise: removing unknown bases from the sequences. There are many different ways to do this, but the simplest is probably using the re.sub() function from the regular expression module to replace all non-ATGC characters with an empty string. As before, we don't want to change the header, so we pass in the do_nothing() function as the third argument to fasta_copy():

```
import re
def remove(dna):
    return re.sub(r'[^ATGCatgc]', '', dna)

fasta_copy('sequences.fasta', 'corrected.fasta', do_nothing, remove)
```

The third bit of the exercise involves changing spaces to underscores in the headers, so our strategy here is the other way around – we want to leave the sequences unchanged, so we supply do_nothing() as the fourth argument, and write a replacement function to process the headers:

```
def fix_spaces(header):
    return header.replace(' ', '_')

fasta_copy('sequences.fasta', 'corrected.fasta', fix_spaces, do_nothing)
```

Similarly, for the fourth bit of the exercise, we write a function to truncate the headers, and pass it to our fasta_copy() function as the third argument:

```
def truncate(header):
    return header[0:10]

fasta_copy('sequences.fasta', 'corrected.fasta', truncate, do_nothing)
```

Looking at the next bit of the exercise, we run up against the limitations of our current implementation of `fasta_copy()`. We're being asked to write a function that appends the length of the sequence to the header, so that this record in the input:

```
>normal_sequence
ACTGGCATGCATCGTACGTACGATCGATCATGCGATGCTACGATCGACGTGTATATCC
```

becomes this in the output:

```
>normal_sequence_58
ACTGGCATGCATCGTACGTACGATCGATCATGCGATGCTACGATCGACGTGTATATCC
```

The trouble is that in order to do this, our `process_header()` function needs to have access to the sequence as well as the header. In other words, both the header and the sequence need to be passed to `process_header()` as arguments, which they currently are not. To make the necessary modifications, we need to change the location of our `process_header()` function call to the point where the sequence is known. We also have to pass in both the header and sequence as arguments:

```python
def fasta_copy(source, destination, process_header, process_sequence):
    output = open(destination, "w")
    header = ""
    for line in open(source):
        if line.startswith('>'):
            header = line.rstrip("\n")[1:]
        else:
            sequence = process_sequence(line.rstrip("\n"))
            new_header = process_header(header, sequence)
            output.write('>' + new_header +"\n")
            output.write(sequence + "\n")
```

copy_fasta.py

Chapter 5: Functional Python

Unfortunately, this will break both of our existing header modification functions (`fix_spaces()` and `truncate()`), because they only expect one argument. If we want them to keep working, we'll have to rewrite them to take two arguments[1] (and simply ignore the second one):

```
def fix_spaces(header, sequence):
    return header.replace(' ', '_')

def truncate(header, sequence):
    return header[0:10]
```

Now back to the problem: appending the sequence length to the header. Here's our header processing function and a call to `fasta_copy` that uses it:

```
def append_len(header, sequence):
    return header + '_' + str(len(sequence))

fasta_copy('sequences.fasta', 'corrected.fasta', append_len, do_nothing)
```

Looking at the first few lines of *corrected.fasta* shows us that it's working:

```
>normal_sequence_58
ACTGGCATGCATCGTACGTACGATCGATCATGCGATGCTACGATCGACGTGTATATCC
>sequence_in_lowercase_50
actgatcatcatcactcgatcgactactatcgatgtcgatctcatcgtag
...
```

The next problem is very similar – appending the AT content. Because, like all good programmers, we are lazy, let's just reuse our `get_at` function from earlier in the chapter:

---

[1] There are other possible ways to fix this – for example, using introspection to count the number of arguments expected by the process_header function and passing the correct number – but these are much more complicated and well beyond the scope of this exercise.

```
from __future__ import division
def get_at(dna):
        return (dna.count('A') + dna.count('T')) / len(dna)

def append_at(header, sequence):
    return header + '_' + str(get_at(sequence))

fasta_copy('sequences.fasta', 'corrected.fasta', append_at, do_nothing)
```

The final bit of the exercise involves a slightly longer header modification function which uses a regular expression to check whether the header should be changed, but it's still quite easy to read:

```
def check_trans(header, sequence):
    if re.search(r'^ATG.*A{5,}$', sequence):
        return header + ' (putative transcript)'
    else:
        return header

fasta_copy('sequences.fasta', 'corrected.fasta', check_trans, do_nothing)
```

Before we leave this exercise, let's make a couple of modifications to our `fasta_copy()` function to make it a bit easier to use. It seems likely that most of the time we'll be using our function to modify either the headers, or the sequences, but rarely both. It makes sense, therefore to set a default value of `do_nothing()` for both the header modification function and the sequence modification function:

```
def fasta_copy(source, destination, process_header=do_nothing,
    process_sequence=do_nothing):
    ...
```

This way, when we call the `fasta_copy()` function we only have to supply functions for the things we want to change using keyword arguments – for example, our solution for the last bit of the exercise becomes:

Chapter 5: Functional Python

```
fasta_copy('sequences.fasta', 'corrected.fasta',
    process_header=check_trans)
```

And we can even simply copy FASTA records without modifying anything by omitting both the `process_header` and the `process_sequence` arguments:

```
fasta_copy('from.fasta', 'to.fasta')
```

Finally, because the `do_nothing()` function is so small, we can replace it with a lambda expression. This means that if we want to reuse the `fasta_copy()` function in another piece of code, we don't have to worry about either including the `do_nothing()` function, or making sure that it's defined before `fasta_copy()`. This modification makes the first line of the `fasta_copy()` definition bigger – here I've written it over several lines for readability:

```
def fasta_copy(
  source,
  destination,
  process_header=lambda x: x,
  process_sequence=lambda x: x
  ):
    ...
```

copy_fasta.py

but it also means that `fasta_copy()` is now a self-contained bit of code which doesn't rely on any other functions being defined.

6: Iterators, comprehensions & generators

Defining lists

Take a look back at the chapter on functional programming, and you'll notice that the bulk of the text talks about functions for manipulating lists of elements. This is not too surprising – the functional style of programming lends itself well to operations on lists of data. Also remember that in Python many things can be considered a lists: dicts are lists of key/value pairs, strings are lists of characters, files are lists of lines, etc.

Looking back at `map()` and `filter()` specifically, it's clear that what we are doing when we use those functions is **defining lists** (although not necessarily creating them: recall that, in Python 3 at least, the `map()` operation is lazy so elements are not created until they are needed). For example, when we write this bit of code:

```
dna_list = ['TAGC', 'ACGTATGC', 'ATG', 'ACGGCTAG']
at_contents = map(get_at, dna_list)
```

we are defining the list `at_contents` as being the result of calling the `get_at function()` on the elements of `dna_list`. Similarly, when we write:

```
long_dna = filter(is_long, dna_list)
```

we are defining the list `long_dna` as being the elements of `dna_list` for which the function `is_long()` returns `True`.

Chapter 6: Iterators, comprehensions & generators

Lists and iterables

Actually, it's not quite true to say that, for each of these examples, that we're defining a list. What we're actually defining is an *iterable object*; in other words, an object that can *behave* like a list insofar as we can iterate over it. We know from previous experience that lists, strings and files are all iterable objects (because we know that we can use them in `for` loops). Many types of Python objects also have methods that return iterable objects (we usually say that they return iterators); for example, the `keys()` method of a dict[1], or the `re.finditer()` method.

To this list of iterable objects we can add the results of calling `map()` and `filter()`. These two functions are interesting because they **take** an iterable object as one of their arguments, and they also **return** an iterable object. So we can, for example, use `map()` to process characters in a string, then pass the resulting iterable object straight to a call to `filter()`:

```
first = map(lambda x : x.upper(), 'abcdef')
second = filter(lambda x : x in ['A', 'B'], first)
```

The important thing to notice about the above code is that we don't care exactly what type of iterable object `first()` is. It could be a list, or an iterator, or something else entirely. All that matters is that `first()` is iterable and can therefore be passed to the `filter()` function.

It turns out that the combination of `map()` and `filter()` in this way is pretty common, and Python has a special type of syntax for defining lists in this way. These special expressions are called *comprehensions*.

---

[1] The exact kind of iterable object returned by `keys()` depends on the version. In Python 2 it returns a list, whereas in Python 3 it returns an iterator.

List comprehensions

List comprehensions allow us to define a list just like we would using the `map()` function. Syntactically, list comprehensions resemble a back to front `for` loop. Here's an example of a list comprehension that defines the list of lengths of sequences in the `dna_list` variable:

```
dna_list = ['TAGC', 'ACGTATGC', 'ATG', 'ACGGCTAG']
lengths = [len(dna) for dna in dna_list]
```

list_comprehension.py

Compare the list comprehension above with the equivalent `for` loop:

```
dna_list = ['TAGC', 'ACGTATGC', 'ATG', 'ACGGCTAG']
lengths = []
for dna in dna_list:
    lengths.append(len(dna))
```

When writing the `for` loop, we write `for dna in dna_list` first, then carry out some processing on the loop variable in the body (`len(dna)`) and append the result to the final list. When writing the same expression as a list comprehension, we write the processing part first, then `for dna in dna_list`, and enclose the whole thing in square brackets. Just as with lambda expressions, the processing part of a list comprehension has to be a single expression. For completeness, here's the same code expressed as a `map()` (we've already seen this code in the functional programming chapter):

```
dna_list = ['TAGC', 'ACGTATGC', 'ATG', 'ACGGCTAG']
lengths = map(len, dna_list)
```

Let's look at a couple more examples that we've already seen how to write using `map()`. Here's a list comprehension that defines a list of the AT contents of the DNA sequences:

Chapter 6: Iterators, comprehensions & generators

```
dna_list = ['TAGC', 'ACGTATGC', 'ATG', 'ACGGCTAG']
ats = [dna.count('A') + dna.count('T')) / len(dna) for dna in dna_list]
```

The expression which calculates the AT content for a single element is exactly the same as we have used before, but when we write it this way we don't have to put it in a function or a lambda expression.

Here's a list comprehension that defines a list of the first one hundred thousand powers of two:

```
l = [2 ** x for x in range(100000)]
```

Compared to the map solution:

```
l = list(range(100000))
m = map(lambda x : 2 ** x, l)
```

the list comprehension is much more readable.

Comprehensions with conditions

The real power of list comprehensions becomes apparent when we use them to map and filter at the same time. To do this, we just add an `if` expression at the end of the comprehension to specify the elements that we want. Here's a list comprehension that defines the list of lengths of all DNA sequences that start with A:

```
dna_list = ['TAGC', 'ACGTATGC', 'ATG', 'ACGGCTAG']
lengths = [len(dna) for dna in dna_list if dna.startswith('A')]
```

Notice that, because we want to use the DNA sequence itself and not the length in the condition, we couldn't achieve the same effect by using `filter()` on a list of lengths. Conditions in a list comprehension need to be a single expression (just like when we are writing a lambda expression), so if we want to implement a condition that requires several statements, we can just wrap it up in a function, then call the function in the condition. For example, to generate a list of lengths of DNA sequences whose AT content is less than 0.6:

```
from __future__ import division
dna_list = ['TAGC', 'ACGTATGC', 'ATG', 'ACGGCTAG']

def is_at_poor(dna):
    at = (dna.count('A') + dna.count('T')) / len(dna)
    return at < 0.6

at_poor_dna_lengths = [len(dna) for dna in dna_list if is_at_poor(dna)]
```

at_comprehension_filter.py

For most applications, the choice of whether to use list comprehensions or `map()`/`filter()` is a personal, stylistic one. List comprehensions are generally considered more "Pythonic" and there's no doubt that they can be easy to read while still performing quite complex operations. For example, here's a list comprehension that defines the list of sequence headers from a FASTA file. It works by using a condition to select just the lines that start with a greater-than symbol, then taking everything after the first character:

```
[line[1:] for line in open('sequences.fasta') if line.startswith('>')]
```

fasta_comprehension.py

Generator expressions

One drawback to using list comprehensions over `map()` and `filter()` is that they are not lazy[1]. Happily, Python has a built in lazy equivalent to the list comprehension called the *generator expression*. The syntax is

---

1   See the section on `map()` in the chapter on functional programming for an explanation of what laziness is and why it's a good thing.

Chapter 6: Iterators, comprehensions & generators

exactly the same, but it uses parentheses rather than square brackets. Here's our long-running `map` example from before, written as first a list comprehension, then as a generator expression:

```
# this statement takes several minutes to execute
l = [2 ** x for x in range(100000)]
# this statement takes no time at all to execute
l = (2 ** x for x in range(100000))
```

An important difference between list comprehensions and generator expressions, and one that will cause trouble if you forget it, is that generator expressions are *exhaustible*; in other words, you can only iterate over them **once**. We've encountered the same behaviour before with file objects – once you iterate over the lines in a file, you cannot iterate over them again without re-opening the file. Be careful not to write code that iterates over the same generator multiple times, as it will probably not do what you want:

```
gen = (x * 2 for x in range(5))
for i in gen:
    print(i) # this line runs five times
# now the generator is exhausted
for i in gen:
    print(i) # this line never runs as there are no more elements in gen
```

Nested comprehensions

We'll finish our survey of list comprehensions by taking a quick look at one final feature: we can use them to iterate over multiple variables at once by adding extra `for` expressions. This is the exact equivalent of using nested `for` loops in procedural code. For example, we can generate a list of all possible dinucleotides by iterating over a list of bases twice (once using the `base1` variable and once using the `base2` variable) and concatenating the two bases at each iteration:

```
bases = ['A', 'T', 'G', 'C']
dn = [base1 + base2 for base1 in bases for base2 in bases]
# dn is now ['AA', 'AT', 'AG', 'AC', 'TA', 'TT', 'TG', 'TC', ...]
```

This is particularly handy for expressing a very common bioinformatics theme: pairwise processing of objects. Imagine we have a list of objects (representing DNA sequences, protein domains, experimental conditions, etc.) and a function (we'll call it `process()`) that will take two such objects as arguments and return the result of running some analysis on them. Using a list comprehension, we can collect the result of running the function on each possible pair of different objects in one expression:

```
r = [
    process(a, b)
    for a in object_list
    for b in object_list
    if a != b
    ]
```

Note how we need to use a condition as part of the comprehension to avoid processing an object with itself.

Dictionary comprehensions

As I pointed out previously, dictionaries can be thought of as simple lists of key/value pairs (with the special ability that the value for a given key can be looked up very quickly), so it makes sense that there's an analogous type of comprehension for defining them. The expression has to be represented as key:value, and the whole comprehension is surrounded by curly brackets:

```
d = {x:x+1 for x in range(10) if x > 5}
# d is now {8: 9, 9: 10, 6: 7, 7: 8}
```

Chapter 6: Iterators, comprehensions & generators

There's no lazy equivalent for a dictionary comprehension (if you think about it, the idea doesn't really make sense since you'd have to evaluate the whole dict as soon as you want to look up a single value).

Dict comprehensions can be useful when we want to pre-calculate some bit of data for each element in a list and then rapidly look up the bit of data corresponding to one particular element. For example, here's how we'd define a dict where the keys are DNA sequences and the values are AT contents using our function defined earlier:

```
from __future__ import division

dna_list = ['TAGC', 'ACGTATGC', 'ATG', 'ACGGCTAG']
def get_at(dna):
    return (dna.count('A') + dna.count('T')) / len(dna)

d = { x : get_at(x) for x in dna_list }
#d is {'ACGTATGC': 0.5, 'ATG': 0.66, 'ACGGCTAG': 0.375, 'TAGC': 0.5}
```

dict_comprehension.py

We have to be remember, when doing this, that we'll get one key/value pair in the resulting dict for each **unique** DNA sequence in the input list. Any duplicate values will simply be overridden.

Another very useful thing we can do with dict comprehensions is to define a dict which allows us to rapidly look up an object based on one of its properties. Imagine we have a list of **DNASequence** objects[1], each of which has a **name** field, and all the name fields are unique. We can create a **name->object** dict like this:

```
name2object = { d.name : d for d in list_of_dna_objects }
```

which will allow us to retrieve the whole **DNASequence** object simply by knowing the **name**:

---
1   See the chapter on object oriented programming for an implementation of this.

```
my_object = name2object.get('ABC123')
```

Set comprehensions

We encountered sets in the chapter on complex data structures. Like a list, each element in a set is a single item, but like a dict, elements have to be unique. Internally, set elements are stored in a way that allows us to check for the existence of an item in a set very rapidly.

We write set comprehensions in exactly the same way as list comprehensions, but using curly brackets rather than square ones:

```
even_integers = {x for x in range(1000) if x % 2 == 0}
```

For example, we can create a set of all the DNA sequences in a list that are longer than 100 base pairs:

```
long_dna = {d for d in dna_list if len(d) > 100}
```

We could, of course, create a list of the DNA sequences rather than a set:

```
long_dna = [d for d in dna_list if len(d) > 100]
```

but if the resulting list had a very large number of elements, checking to see whether a particular DNA sequence was in it could become very slow, whereas with a set the same operation is very fast regardless of the number of elements.

Iterators and generators

We've seen, in this chapter and the last, that iterable types (things like strings, lists and dicts) are extremely useful in Python. We can iterate over their elements using `for` loops; we can process them using functional tools like `map()` and `filter()`, and we can use them to

Chapter 6: Iterators, comprehensions & generators

define new data structures using comprehensions. Given that iteration is such a powerful idea, we might want to use it in our own code: in other words, we might want to create our own *iterable types*.

The most basic mechanism for doing this is the `iterator` interface[1]. To make use of the iterator interface, we have to give our class a method with the special name `__iter__()` (the word `iter` surrounded by double underscores) which returns an iterator. We can get an iterator for built in classes like strings by called the `iter()` function on them[2]. So for very simple cases where iterating over the object is just a case of iterating over one of its variables, we can implement `__iter__()` by just returning the iterator of the variable that holds the data. Here's an example using a simplified version of the `DNASequence` class from the chapter on object oriented programming:

```
class DNASequence():
    sequence = 'atgccgcat'

    def __iter__(self):    ❶
        return iter(self.sequence)

my_seq = DNASequence()
for base in my_seq:    ❷
    print(base)
```

iterator.py

In the `__iter__()` method❶, we simply return the iterator supplied by the `sequence` string variable. The presence of the `__iter__()` method is what allows us to iterate over the `DNASequence` directly❷. If we didn't have the `__iter__()` method, we'd have to iterate over the `sequence` variable explicitly like this:

---

1 Since this section uses class definitions, it's a good idea to make sure you've read the chapter on object oriented programming if you haven't already.
2 Notice that the difference between the built in `iter()` function, and the `__iter__()` method that we give to our class – the latter is surrounded by double underscores.

Chapter 6: Iterators, comprehensions & generators

```
for base in my_seq.sequence:
    print(base)
```

The first approach, using __iter__(), is better not just because it involves less typing, but because it doesn't rely on the implementation details. We could change the way that the sequence is stored in the class (for example, changing the name of the variable) and as long as we altered the __iter__() method, lines of code like

```
for base in my_seq:
```

would continue to work.

Let's now look at a slightly more sophisticated example; what if we wanted our object to iterate over **codons** rather than individual bases? To do this, we need to look in a little more detail about what an iterator actually is. The definition is quite simple: an iterator is just an object that implements a next() method[1]. The next() method, when called, has to return the next element in the sequence or, if the end of the sequence has been reached, raise a StopIteration exception[2]. For our case, the easiest thing to do is to turn the DNASequence class into an iterator by implementing a next() method, and modify the __iter__() method to simply return the object itself:

---

1 In Python 3, the name of the method has been changed to __next__().
2 See the chapter on exceptions for details of how this works.

Chapter 6: Iterators, comprehensions & generators

```
class DNASequence():
    position = 0
    sequence = 'atgccgcat'

    def __iter__(self):
        return self

    def next(self): ❶
        if self.position < (len(self.sequence) - 2): ❷
            codon = self.sequence[self.position:self.position+3]
            self.position += 3
            return codon
        else:
            raise StopIteration
my_seq = DNASequence()
for codon in my_seq:
    print(codon)
```

codon_iterator.py

The above code is quite complicated, so let's take a look at it step by step. The job of the **next()** method❶ is to return the next element in the sequence (i.e. the next codon). To do that, it needs an extra variable – **position** – which keeps track of the current position in the sequence. If there are at least three bases remaining after the current position❷ we extract them, add three to the position and then return the codon. If, however, the current position is within two bases of the end of the sequence, then we have reached the end and there are no more elements to return, so we tell Python to stop iterating❸. If we look at the output from this code then we can see that the individual elements when iterating over a **DNASequence** are now codons rather than individual bases:

```
atg
ccg
cat
```

Although this solution takes care of hiding the complexity of codon iteration inside the object, it's not very satisfactory. In the real world, we are likely to want to iterate over an object in multiple different ways. For example, with our **DNASequence** object we might want to iterate over individual bases, codons, or kmers of a specified length. Happily, Python provides a simple mechanism for multiple iteration: *generators*.

A generator is like a method, but instead of using the **return** keyword to return a single result, it uses the **yield** keyword to return results one at a time. We can see how generators work by looking at a familiar example – a method that returns overlapping 4mers from an input sequence. Here's a normal method that carries out the job:

```
def get_4mers(dna):
    4mers = []
    for i in range(len(dna) - 3):
        4mers.append(dna[i:i+4])
    return 4mers
```

And here's the same idea written as a generator:

```
def generate_4mers(dna):
    for i in range(len(dna) - 3):
        yield dna[i:i+4]

for x in generate_4mers('actggcgtgcatg'):
    print(x)
```

generator.py

Notice how the result of calling **generate_4mers** is **not** a list of 4mers, but rather an iterator that will iterate over the resulting list when used in a **for** loop (or a **map()**, or a **filter()**, or a comprehension, etc.). Arguably, the generator version is much easier to read; it's also much more memory efficient as it only has to store a single 4mer at a time.

Chapter 6: Iterators, comprehensions & generators

Now we've seen how generators work, we can rewrite our **DNASequence** example to take advantage of them. Here's a **DNASequence** class which allows three types of iteration – by base, by codon, or by kmer:

```
class DNASequence():

    sequence = 'atgccgcat'

    def bases(self):
        return iter(self.sequence)

    def codons(self):
        for i in range(0, len(self.sequence) -2, 3):
            yield self.sequence[i:i+3]

    def kmers(self, k):
        for i in range(len(self.sequence) - k +1):
            yield self.sequence[i:i+k]

my_seq = DNASequence()
for base in my_seq.bases():
    print(base)
for codon in my_seq.codons():
    print(codon)
for kmer in my_seq.kmers(5):
    print(kmer)
```

multiple_generators.py

The **bases()** method uses the simple approach to iteration we saw earlier, whereas the **codons()** and **kmers()** method use generators. Notice that we have to supply an argument to the **kmers()** method to tell it what value of k we want. This version of the **DNASequence** class has the benefit that the processing code (outside the class definition) is extremely readable, and the output shows that everything is working as expected:

```
a
t
g
c
c
g
c
a
t
atg
ccg
cat
atgcc
tgccg
gccgc
ccgca
cgcat
```

Recap

We started this chapter by giving a little bit of extra context to our previous look at functional programming, and saw that often what we are interested in is defining sequences of data. We then looked at how, in many cases, Python's special list comprehension syntax could replace `map()` and `filter()` in a concise and readable way. We then extended the basic idea to look at comprehensions for other data types – dicts and sets – along with a lazy equivalent for lists.

Finally, we saw how to exploit the power of Python's sophisticated iteration system for our own classes and objects, allowing us to encapsulate the complexities of iteration inside objects and write cleaner, more readable code.

Exercises

BLAST processor

Rewrite your solutions to the **BLAST processor** exercises from the previous chapter to use list comprehensions. Here's a reminder of the questions we want to answer:

- How many hits have fewer than 20 mismatches?

- List the subject sequence names for the ten matches with the lowest percentage of identical positions

- For matches where the subject sequence name includes the string "COX1", list the start position on the query as a proportion of the length of the match

Primer search

Write a generator which will generate all possible primers of a given length (hint: look back at the chapter on recursion for an example of a function that will act as a starting point). Write a second generator which uses the first to generate all possible pairs of such primers.

Solutions

BLAST processor

This is a pretty straightforward exercise – we're just taking our solutions to a previous set of problems and expressing them in a different way. However, it's a very useful one to do, as seeing comprehensions and `map()`/`filter()` side by side is a great way to explore the differences in syntax. For each of the code samples below I'll show the `map()`/`filter()` solution first, followed by the equivalent comprehension.

First of all, recall that we have to filter out lines that start with "#" as these lines contain comments rather than BLAST hit data. Our original solution used `filter()`, but the same logic applies nicely to the list comprehension solution:

```
# filtering out comment lines using a function and filter
def comment_filter(line):
    return not line.startswith('#')

hit_lines = filter(comment_filter, open('blast_result.txt'))

# filtering out comment lines using a list comprehension
hit_lines = [l for l in open('blast_result.txt') if not
l.startswith('#')]
```

blast_filter.py

Notice that the expression that gets evaluated for each lines is just the line itself (l), since for this comprehension we don't want to alter the lines at all.

Now we can tackle the first question. In our original solution we used `filter()` to select only the hit lines where the fifth element after

Chapter 6: Iterators, comprehensions & generators

splitting (i.e. the number of mismatches) was less than 20. For the new solution, we apply exactly the same logic using a comprehension:

```
# selecting low-mismatch hits using a filter function
def mismatch_filter(hit_string):
    mismatch_count = int(hit_string.split("\t")[4])
    return mismatch_count < 20
f = filter(mismatch_filter, hit_lines)
print(len(f))

# selecting low-mismatch hits using a list comprehension
few_mismatch_hits = [ l for l in hit_lines if int(l.split("\t")[4]) < 20
]
print(len(few_mismatch_hits))
```

On to the second question. In our original solution this was a three-part process: sort the list of hits by percent ID, take the first ten elements, then extract the subject string using a `map()`. For the new solution, the first step is the same, but we can do the last two using a single list comprehension:

```
# get subject names for the ten hits with the lowest percent id

def get_subject(hit_string):
    return hit_string.split("\t")[1]

hits_sorted_by_percent_id = sorted(hit_lines, key=get_percent_id)
low_id_hits = hits_sorted_by_percent_id[0:10]
for subject in map(get_subject, low_id_hits):
    print(subject)

# same using a list comprehension
subjects = [ l.split("\t")[1] for l in hits_sorted_by_percent_id[0:10] ]
print(subjects)
```

The final question involves both a `filter()` and a `map()`. First we select the hits where the subject name contains the string "COX1", then we map those lines to their ratio of query start position to hit length. We can fit the whole thing into a single list comprehension – below I've split the comprehension over multiple lines to make it easier to read:

```
# solution using filter and map
# this requires the following two functions
def cox1_filter(hit_string):
    subject = hit_string.split("\t")[1]
    if "COX1" in subject:
        return True
    else:
        return False

def start_ratio(hit_string):
    query_start = int(hit_string.split("\t")[6])
    hit_length = int(hit_string.split("\t")[3])
    return query_start / hit_length

cox1_hits = filter(cox1_filter, hit_lines)
for ratio in map(start_ratio, cox1_hits):
    print(ratio)

# solution using a list comprehension
# none of the functions above are used
ratios = [
    int(l.split("\t")[6]) / int(l.split("\t")[3])
    for l in hit_lines
    if "COX1" in l.split("\t")[1]
]
print(ratios)
```

blast_filter.py

Primer search

Since the interesting part of this exercise is not the generation of possible primers *per se*, but the use of generators, we'll start with the recursive kmer generating program from the chapter on recursion. Let's remind ourselves of what it looks like:

Chapter 6: Iterators, comprehensions & generators

```
def generate_primers(length):
    if length == 1:
        return ['A', 'T', 'G', 'C']
    else:
        result = []
        for seq in generate_primers(length - 1):
            for base in ['A', 'T', 'G', 'C']:
                result.append(seq + base)
        return result
```

We won't go into the details of how it works – you'll find an in-depth look at the implementation in the chapter on recursion. Instead, let's concentrate on the result that is produced. We know that the output from this function is a list of all possible combinations of the four DNA bases of a given length, which allows us to make some confident predictions about the size of the output. The number of elements in the returned list will be four raised to the power of the sequence length. So, a call to `generate_primers(3)` will return a list with 64 elements, but if we double the length to 6 then we'll get over four thousand elements in the returned list, and if we double it again to 12 we get over sixteen million elements. For realistic primer lengths of around twenty bases, the number of elements in the returned list is on the order of one trillion, which is obviously not going to fit into memory[1].

This function, therefore, is a good candidate for being rewritten as a generator. If we can do that, then we'll only ever have to store a single element in memory at any one time. Remarkably, converting this function to a generator requires very few changes. We simply replace each instance where we return a value, or add a new element to the result list, to a `yield` statement:

---

1   Of course, any program that attempts to carry out any kind of processing on a list of one trillion elements is probably going to be prohibitively slow regardless of how the elements are generated, but we'll overlook that for this example.

```
def generate_primers(length):
    if length == 1:
        for base in ['A', 'T', 'G', 'C']:
            yield(base)
    else:
        for seq in generate_primers(length - 1):
            for base in ['A', 'T', 'G', 'C']:
                yield(seq+base)
```

primer_search.py

The nice thing about this transformation from a list-returning function to a generator is that it's completely transparent to any code which calls this function. If we have, elsewhere in our program, a line that looks like this:

```
for primer in generate_primers(15):
    # process a single primer
```

The magic of iteration will ensure that it continues to run as before, even though the return value of `generate_primers()` is no longer a list but a generator.

Now we can tackle the final bit of this problem: writing another generator whose job is to generate all possible pairs of primers. It's surprisingly straightforward: we just iterate over all possible forward primers, and all possible reverse primers, and `yield` each pair as a tuple in turn:

```
def generate_pairs(length):
    for forward in generate_primers(length):
        for reverse in generate_primers(length):
            yield(forward, reverse)
```

primer_search.py

Just as before, writing this as a generator rather than a list-returning function ensures that only one pair needs to be stored in memory at a time, but we can still write code that treats the list of pairs just like a list:

Chapter 6: Iterators, comprehensions & generators

```
for f,r in generate_pairs(9):
    # do something with f and r
```

One final note: the problem of generating all possible combinations of letters from a fixed alphabet (of which this exercise is an example) is quite a common problem in programming, so there's a built in Python module to handle it. The `itertools.product()` function takes a list of tokens and a repeat number, and generates a sequence of tuples containing every possible sequence of tokens for the given length:

```
for seq in itertools.product('ATGC', repeat=3):
    print(seq)
```

```
('A', 'A', 'A')
('A', 'A', 'T')
('A', 'A', 'G')
('A', 'A', 'C')
('A', 'T', 'A')
('A', 'T', 'T')
('A', 'T', 'G')
('A', 'T', 'C')
...
```

Of course, for this particular question we want the bases joined together to make a DNA sequence:

```
for seq in itertools.product('ATGC', repeat=3):
    print(''.join(seq))
```

```
AAA
AAT
AAG
AAC
ATA
ATT
ATG
ATC
AGA
...
```

which, to bring this discussion full circle, we can do using a list comprehension!

```
[''.join(seq) for seq in itertools.product('ATGC', repeat=3)]
```

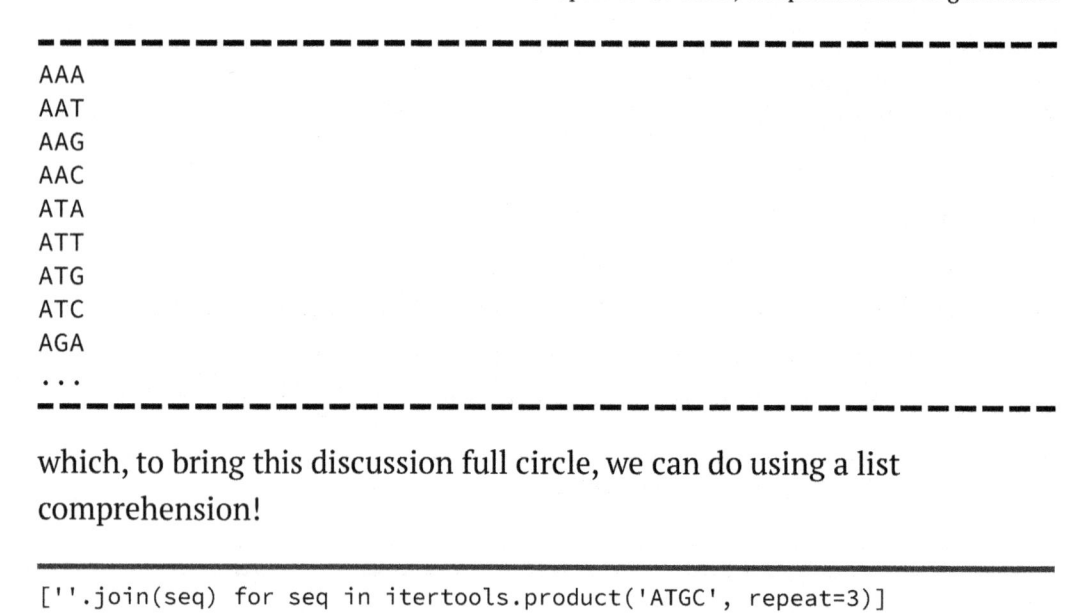

7: Exception handling

Something that becomes clear depressingly quickly when we first start to learn to code is that our programs often don't behave exactly as we like. Several different types of problems occur. There are straightforward *syntax errors*, where we forget a colon or accidentally leave a line unindented:

```
for base in dna
print(base)
```

As we know from experience, syntax errors will prevent our program from running at all.

There are also typos and incorrect function and variable names, and things like trying to use an integer as a string:

```
print(dna.converttouppercase)
print('abc' + 3)
```

These are different from syntax errors because they will not stop the program running entirely, but they will cause it to exit with an error message when it reaches that point in the code.

Then there are bugs – more subtle errors that will not prevent the program from running or create an error message, but will not do quite what you want:

```
dna = 'atctgcatattgcgtctgatg'
a_count = dna.count('A') #whoops, the sequence is in lower case
```

What all these types of errors have in common is that they are an intrinsic property of the code. In other words, if we run a piece of code that contains one of these errors then we'll encounter the same problem every time in a very predictable way.

However, there's another class of errors that are not intrinsic to the code, but instead are the result of some external situation. For example, consider the common error that you get when you try to open a file that doesn't exist:

```
IOError: [Errno 2] No such file or directory: 'missing.txt'
```

This error is not a property of the code, but of the environment in which it is being run. If we were to take the exact same piece of code that caused the error and run it at a different time[1] or in a different folder it might run perfectly well. In programming, we refer to situations like this as *exceptions*, and Python's built in mechanism for handling them is called *exception handling*[2].

A quick note before we dive in: the first section of this chapter uses a rather boring non-biological example to illustrate how to use exceptions. That's because, for reasons that will become clear later on in the chapter, it's easier to get to grips with the basic exception system using built in functions. Later in the chapter we switch to biological examples.

Catching exceptions

The "No such file" message is what the user of a program will see if the code tries to open a non-existent file. The message is part of Python's response to an exception (the program stopping is another part of the response). It's relatively helpful for the programmer, as it identifies the

---

1 i.e. after we had created the missing file.
2 Exception handling is useful for dealing with many other situations as well, but we'll come to those later in the chapter.

Chapter 7: Exception handling

exact error that occurred, but it's not very helpful for the user. If we're writing a program that reads data from files, we might want to intercept, or *catch*, the exception that caused the error message to be printed and handle it in the code. To catch an exception, we enclose the bit of the code that has the potential to cause the exception (in this case, the `open()` function) in a `try` block, and add the code that we want to run in the case of an exception in an `except` block:

```
try:
    f = open('misssing.txt')
    print('file contents: ' + f.read())
except:
    print("sorry, couldn't find the file")
```

`try_excpet.py`

`try` and `except` blocks work just like the `for`/`if`/function blocks that we're already familiar with – they end with a colon and the lines inside them are indented. When we run the above code, the lines in the `try` block are executed and if one of them causes an exception, the program jumps directly to the `except` block and starts executing the code there. In the above code, the `open()` function call will create an exception when the file is not found (we say that the `open()` function *raises* an exception) and so the `print()` line will not be executed. Because we have caught the exception, we don't get the usual error message; instead, our customized error message is printed:

```
sorry, couldn't find the file
```

There's another important effect of catching the exception: rather than our program terminating, as normally happens when Python encounters an error, it will continue running at a point after the `try`/`except` blocks.

This allows the program to try to recover from the error. If we add a line of code at the end of our example:

```
try:
    f = open('misssing')
    print('file contents: ' + f.read())
except:
    print("sorry, couldn't find the file")
print("continuing....")
```

and re-run it, we'll see that execution continues:

```
sorry, couldn't find the file
continuing...
```

Catching specific errors

There's one problem with the above approach to handling errors: it catches **any** kind of exception and responds to it in the same way. Consider this bit of code that reads the contents of a file, turns it into an integer, then adds five and prints the result:

```
try:
    f = open('my_file.txt')      ❶
    my_number = int(f.read())    ❷
    print(my_number + 5)
except:
    print("sorry, couldn't find the file")
```

Now there are two possible situations that could cause an exception: the file could be missing (in which case we will get a `IOError` when we try to open it❶) or the contents could be a string that can't be parsed into an integer (in which case we'll get a `ValueError` when we try to convert it❷). What happens if we create a new file called *my_file.txt* which contains the text "twenty-three" and run the code? The call to `int()` will

Chapter 7: Exception handling

raise a `ValueError`, which will get caught by the `except` block and we will see the very misleading error message:

```
sorry, couldn't find the file
```

What we need is a way of specifying that our `except` block is only intended to handle one specific type of exception: an `IOError`. Happily, it's very easy to do this in Python – we just give the type of error as part of the `except` block definition:

```
try:
    f = open('my_file.txt')
    my_number = int(f.read())
    print(my_number + 5)
except IOError:
    print("sorry, couldn't find the file")
```

Now when we run the code with our *my_file.txt* present the exception, which is a `ValueError`, is **not** handled by our `except` block, and causes the correct default error message to be printed:

```
ValueError: invalid literal for int() with base 10: 'twenty-
three\n'
```

but we still get our custom error message if the file is missing.

We can make our code even better by writing separate `except` blocks for the two possible errors. We just place the `except` blocks one after another:

Chapter 7: Exception handling

```
try:
    f = open('my_file.txt')
    my_number = int(f.read())
    print(my_number + 5)
except IOError:
    print("sorry, couldn't find the file")
except ValueError:
    print("sorry, couldn't parse the number")
```

exception_types.py

This is a very powerful technique, as it allows us to write code that can respond appropriately to many different types of error. If we still want to write an `except` block that handles multiple types of exception then we just write them as a tuple[1]:

```
try:
    f = open('my_file.txt')
    my_number = int(f.read())
    print(my_number + 5)
except (IOError, ValueError):
    print("sorry, something went wrong")
```

In the above examples, we've limited ourselves to printing out error message in the `except` blocks but we can use `except` blocks to run any kind of code. For instance, we could prompt the user to enter a new file name in the event of an `IOError`, or ask them to enter the desired value for `my_number` if there's a `ValueError`. To stop the examples from getting too long, the remaining examples in this chapter will mostly use `print()` statements in `except` blocks. Just remember when you're reading them that `except` blocks can hold arbitrary chunks of code – they can call functions, create objects, or do anything else that normal code can do.

---

1 Take a look at the chapter on complex data structures if you've never heard of tuples before.

Chapter 7: Exception handling

Getting information about the exception

Our error messages in the file-opening-and-parsing example above are still not perfect, because there are multiple different reasons that an exception might occur. For example, trying to open a non-existent file will cause an **IOError**, but so will trying to open a file that you don't have permission to view, or attempting to open a folder rather than a file. The error message that we display to the user would be more helpful if it contained information about the specifics of the exception.

To get hold of that information, we have to remember that an exception is just an object[1] (just like a file object or a regular expression match object). We can access the exception object by making one small addition to our **except** block:

```
except IOError as ex:
```

and we can then use the variable **ex** to refer to the exception object. The details of what we can do with exception objects differ according to the type of exception. For **IOError** exceptions, we can get a string description of the error by referencing the **strerror** field. Here's an updated version of our example that, when handling an **IOError**, prints out the error string as part of the error message:

```
try:
    f = open('my_file.txt')
    my_number = int(f.read())
    print(my_number + 5)
except IOError as ex:
    print("sorry, couldn't open the file: " + ex.strerror)
except ValueError:
    print("sorry, couldn't parse the number")
```

---

1 Consequently, the following explanation will make more sense if you've read the chapter on object oriented programming.

Now when we run the code and encounter an `IOError`, the first part of the error message will always be the same, but the second part will pinpoint the specific nature of the problem:

```
sorry, couldn't open the file: No such file or directory
sorry, couldn't open the file: Permission denied
sorry, couldn't open the file: Is a directory
```

To figure out what properties are available for a given exception class we can consult the Python documentation[1], but there's also a more generic mechanism for getting the details of an error. Exception objects have a field called `args`[2], which is a list of details for the error. For most types of exception, one element of the list will be a string giving details of the problem. For `ValueError` objects, it's the first element, so we can modify our `ValueError` hander thus:

```python
try:
    f = open('my_file.txt')
    my_number = int(f.read())
    print(my_number + 5)
except IOError as ex:
    print("sorry, couldn't find the file: " + ex.strerror)
except ValueError as ex:
    print("sorry, couldn't parse the number: " + ex.args[0])
```

exception_details.py

and when we run the code we'll get a more detailed error as part of our error message if the contents of the file can't be parsed:

```
sorry, couldn't parse the number: invalid literal for int() with base 10: '12.56\n'
```

---

1 http://docs.python.org/2/library/exceptions.html
2 So called because it holds the arguments used to construct the object – see the chapter on object oriented programming for more details on constructors.

Chapter 7: Exception handling

else blocks in exception handling

In the file parsing example we've been looking at above, there are three lines of code in the `try` block. The first line can raise an `IOError` if there's a problem opening the file, and the second line can raise a `ValueError` if there's a problem reading an integer from it. But the third line – where we print a value – might also cause an `IOError`[1]. If this happens, then the exception will be picked up by our first `except` block, and our program will misleadingly inform the user that there was a problem reading the input file.

We can avoid this situation by moving the `print()` line outside the `try` block:

```
try:
    f = open('my_file.txt')
    my_number = int(f.read())
except IOError as ex:
    print("sorry, couldn't find the file: " + ex.strerror)
except ValueError as ex:
    print("sorry, couldn't parse the number: " +  ex.args[0])
print(my_number + 5)
```

but that just brings up a different problem: if there is an error, either in reading the file or parsing the number, then the value of `my_number` will not be set and we won't be able to print it. What we really need is a way of specifying that the `print()` line is **only** to be executed if there wasn't any exception raised in the `try` block. We can do this by placing the code in an `else` block:

---

1   For example, if we are running this bit of code using shell redirection and we run out of space on the output file device.

```
try:
    f = open('my_file.txt')
    my_number = int(f.read())
except IOError as ex:
    print("sorry, couldn't find the file: " + ex.strerror)
except ValueError as ex:
    print("sorry, couldn't parse the number: " +  ex.args[0])
else:
    print(my_number + 5)
```

else.py

The `else` block is run only if there were no exceptions raised in the `try` block. It's a useful technique for a very specific scenario: when we want to run code **only** in the absence of earlier exceptions **without** catching exceptions for the code itself.

finally blocks in exception handling

What if there's a bit of code that we want to run regardless of whether or not an exception was raised? For example, imagine that our program create a temporary file that needs to be deleted when the program exits:

```
import os

# write some temporary data to a file
t = open('temp.txt', 'w')
t.write('some important temporary text')
t.close()

# do some other processing
f = open('my_file.txt')
my_number = int(f.read())
print(my_number + 5)

# delete the temporary file
os.remove('temp.txt')
```

Consider what happens if an exception is raised in the processing steps – the program will exit and the temporary file will not be removed. We can

Chapter 7: Exception handling

rewrite the program using the techniques we learned above to catch the exceptions, but where should we put the clean up code? One solution is to place it at the end of the `try` block and all the `except` blocks:

```
import os
t = open('temp.txt', 'w')
t.write('some important temporary text')
t.close()
try:
    f = open('my_file.txt')
    my_number = int(f.read())
    print(my_number + 5)
    os.remove('temp.txt') # delete the temp file
except IOError as ex:
    print("sorry, couldn't find the file: " + ex.strerror)
    os.remove('temp.txt') # delete the temp file
except ValueError as ex:
    print("sorry, couldn't parse the number: " +  ex.args[0])
    os.remove('temp.txt') # delete the temp file
```

but this isn't a great idea. Not only do we have to repeat the code three times, but it still won't get run in some circumstances – for instance, if an exception is raised inside the `try` block that doesn't get caught by one of our `except` blocks. We could put the clean up code after the `try`/`except` section:

```
import os
t = open('temp.txt', 'w')
t.write('some important temporary text')
t.close()
try:
    f = open('my_file.txt')
    my_number = int(f.read())
    print(my_number + 5)
except IOError as ex:
    print("sorry, couldn't find the file: " + ex.strerror)
except ValueError as ex:
    print("sorry, couldn't parse the number: " +  ex.args[0])

os.remove('temp.txt')
```

Chapter 7: Exception handling

This solves the first problem but not the second – if an exception is raised inside the `try` block and not caught by one of our `except` blocks, the clean up code won't be run.

The correct way to handle this situation in Python is using a `finally` block. A `finally` block is **guaranteed** to run after the `try` block has finished, regardless of whether an exception is raised or not. The `finally` block has to come after the `try`/`except`/`else` blocks:

```
import os
t = open('temp.txt', 'w')
t.write('some important temporary text')
t.close()
try:
    f = open('my_file.txt')
    my_number = int(f.read())
    print(my_number + 5)
except IOError as ex:
    print("sorry, couldn't find the file: " + ex.strerror)
except ValueError as ex:
    print("sorry, couldn't parse the number: " + ex.args[0])
finally:
    os.remove('temp.txt')
```

finally.py

and is the best way to ensure that code is run even in the event of an unhandled exception. `finally` blocks are typically used for cleaning up or releasing resources like threads and database connections.

Blocks of code that use exception handling can become quite complex, so here's a generic example with a quick summary:

Chapter 7: Exception handling

```
try:
    # code in here will be run until an exception is raised
except ExceptionTypeOne:
    # code in here will be run if an ExceptionTypeOne
    # is raised in the try block
except ExceptionTypeTwo:
    # code in here will be run if an ExceptionTypeTwo
    # is raised in the try block
else:
    # code in here will be run after the try block
    # if it doesn't raise an exception
finally:
    # code in here will always be run
```

Context managers

Some common operations are pretty much always carried out inside `try`/`finally` blocks, to ensure that resources used inside the `try` block are released. The most obvious example is reading a file – the pattern is nearly always:

```
f = open('somefile.txt')
try:
    # do something with f
finally:
    f.close()
```

This is to ensure that the file is always closed regardless of any exceptions that might occur while it is open. A feature of Python called *context managers* allows this type of pattern to be encapsulated in a class and reused. Context managers are invoked using the `with` statement. The following bit of code is equivalent to the one above:

```
with open('somefile.txt') as f:
    # do something with f
```

but is a lot more readable. The File context manager is by far the most-used, but there are several other built in context managers, and we can define our own[1].

Nested try/except blocks

Just as we can nest `if` statements or `for` loops in Python, we can nest `try/catch` blocks. This can be useful when we need to access variables in the `except` or `finally` blocks that were defined earlier. Consider the case where we want to ensure that a file is closed properly even in the event of an exception being raised. We might be tempted to write something like this, using the `finally` block technique from above:

```
try:
    f = open('my_file.txt') # this line might raise an IOError
    my_number = int(f.read()) # this line might raise a ValueError
except IOError:
    print('cannot open file!')
except ValueError:
    print('not an integer!')
finally:
    f.close()
```

but that won't work because the variable `f` is created inside the `try` block and so can't be accessed from the `finally` block[2]. To achieve the result we want, we need two nested `try` blocks:

---

1 A discussion of how and why to do this is beyond the scope of this book, but if you're interested, take a look at the `contextlib` module.
2 Recall that in Python, variables which are declared inside a block of any type have their scope limited to that block.

Chapter 7: Exception handling

```
try:
    f = open('my_file.txt')
    try:
        my_number = int(f.read())
    except ValueError:
        print('not an integer!')
    finally:
        f.close()
except IOError:
    print('cannot open file')
```

nested_try.py

Because the inner `finally` block is inside the outer `try` block, it has access to the variable `f`. It's a good idea to use this feature sparingly – if you find yourself writing code that requires more than two layers of nested `try` blocks, then it's probably better to encapsulate some of that complexity inside a separate function.

Exceptions bubble up

Imagine you have some function that calls another function:

```
def function_one:
    # do some processing...
    return 5

def function_two:
    my_number = function_one()
    return my_number + 2

print(function_two())
```

and that the code represented by `do some processing...` could potentially raise an exception. We could catch and handle the exception in `function_one`:

```
def function_one:
    try:
        # do some processing...
        return 5
    except SomeException:
        # handle the exception...

def function_two:
    my_number = function_one()
    return my_number + 2

print(function_two())
```

but what happens if we don't? The answer is that the exception will be passed up to the bit of code that called `function_one` – which in our case is `function_two`. So we have a second chance to handle the exception there:

```
def function_one:
    # do some processing...
    return 5

def function_two:
    try:
        my_number = function_one()
        return my_number + 2
    except SomeException:
        # handle the exception...

print(function_two())
```

And if we don't handle it there, then the exception is passed up again to the top level code, so we have a third chance to handle it:

Chapter 7: Exception handling

```
def function_one:
    # do some processing...
    return 5

def function_two:
    my_number = function_one()
    return my_number + 2
try:
    print(function_two())
except SomeException:
    # handle the exception
```

When describing this behaviour, we often say that exceptions *bubble up*. The best place to handle a given exception depends on what the program is doing, and a discussion of best-practice exception handling is beyond the scope of this book. However, it's often the case that it's easier to handle an exception at a higher level (i.e. in `function_two` or the top level code in our above example). As a general rule, your code should handle exceptions **in the place where it can do something about them**.

Sometimes we want to take some action in response to an exception – for example, print a warning message – but we still want to allow code at a higher level to "see" the exception and respond to it. Python has a handy shorthand for doing this: the statement `raise`, on its own, will cause the exception that's currently being handled to be re-raised. This allows us to write something like this:

```
def function_one:
    try:
        # do some processing...
        return 5
    except SomeException:
        print("warning: something went wrong")
        raise
def function_two:
    my_number = function_one()
    return my_number + 2
try:
    print(function_two())
except SomeException:
    # handle the exception
```

which effectively handles the exception twice: once in `function_one()` and then again at the top level of code. Speaking of the `raise` statement....

Raising exceptions

As we've seen above, exceptions are the way that Python's built in methods and functions signal that something has gone wrong. Writing exception-handling code in the form of `try/except` blocks is our way of intercepting those signals and responding to them.

We can also write our own code that is capable of signalling when something has gone wrong. Just as with built in functions, our own functions can indicate a problem by raising an exception. To do this we create a new exception object, and then use it in a `raise` statement:

```
e = ValueError()
raise e
```

Chapter 7: Exception handling

In object oriented terms, what we are doing here is creating a new instance of the `ValueError` class and then passing it to `raise`. It's more usual to create the exception object and raise it in a single statement:

```
raise ValueError()
```

The error message that we get from the above line of code is very unhelpful:

```
ValueError:
```

because we have not attached any details to our `ValueError` instance. To make it more useful, we can pass a string argument to the `ValueError` constructor describing the problem:

```
raise ValueError("this is a description of the problem")
```

Let's look at a biological example. Take the `get_at_content()` function that we've used many times before: it takes a DNA string as its argument and returns the AT content as a floating point number:

```python
def get_at_content(dna):
    length = len(dna)
    a_count = dna.count('A')
    t_count = dna.count('T')
    at_content = (a_count + t_count) / length
    return at_content
```

This function only works on DNA sequences without any ambiguous bases – it can only handle ATGC nucleotides. So we'll modify it to raise an exception if it's called with an argument that contains non-ATGC bases. We'll use a regular expression to check for non-ATGC bases, and raise a `ValueError` if one is found:

```
import re
def get_at_content(dna):
    if re.search(r'[^ATGC]', dna):
        raise ValueError('Sequence cannot contain non-ATGC bases')
    length = len(dna)
    a_count = dna.count('A')
    t_count = dna.count('T')
    at_content = (a_count + t_count) / length
    return at_content
```

check_bases.py

Now if we attempt to pass in an invalid DNA sequence string to the function:

```
print(get_at_content('ACGTACGTGAC'))
print(get_at_content('ACTGCTNAACT'))
```

it will raise an exception which, if uncaught, will cause the program to exit with an error message:

```
0.454545454545
Traceback (most recent call last):
  ...
ValueError: Sequence cannot contain non-ATGC bases
```

Once we know that this function can potentially raise an exception, we can catch and deal with it in the usual way. For example, if we have a list of sequences for which we want to print the AT content we can catch any exceptions raised by `get_at_content()` to ensure that a single invalid sequence doesn't cause the entire program to crash:

Chapter 7: Exception handling

```
sequences = ['ACGTACGTGAC', 'ACTGCTNAACT', 'ATGGCGCTAGC']
for seq in sequences:
    try:
        print('AT content for ' + seq + ' is ' + str(get_at_content(seq)))
    except ValueError:
        print('skipping invalid sequence '+ seq)
```

In the above code, if we didn't handle the `ValueError` exception, then the second sequence in the list (which contains an `N`) would cause the program to crash and the third sequence would never get processed. Catching the exception allows our program to gracefully deal with the invalid sequence by printing a warning, then carry on processing the list:

```
AT content for ACGTACGTGAC is 0.454545454545
skipping invalid sequence ACTGCTNAACT
AT content for ATGGCGCTAGC is 0.363636363636
```

Custom exception types

There's a fairly obvious problem with using a `ValueError` to indicate an invalid sequence in the example above. If we write an `except` block to catch and handle it, that same `except` block will also catch any other `ValueError` that might be raised. There are lots of operations that can create a `ValueError` in Python, and if one of those occurs somewhere inside the `try` block, our code above will wrongly claim that a given sequence has been skipped because it's invalid. This can lead to big trouble when programming, because it effectively hides other errors, making code very difficult to debug.

The fundamental cause of the problem is that `ValueError` is not **specific** enough. It can be raised in response to a wide variety of situations, so when we encounter a `ValueError` we don't know if it's because of something that happened in `get_at_content()` or something that happened elsewhere. The solution is to create our own exception class to represent a problem with an invalid base. Doing so is very straightforward – we just define a new class which is a subclass of the Exception class[1]. Since the job of our new class is just to carry a message, it doesn't need any members or methods. The body of the class can just be pass[2] and we can rely on the constructor from the Exception superclass:

```
class AmbiguousBaseError(Exception):
    pass
```

We can now edit get_at_content so that it raises an AmbiguousBaseError, and modify our except block so that it only catches an AmbiguousBaseError:

```
def get_at_content(dna):
    if re.search(r'[^ATGC]', dna):
        raise AmbiguousBaseError('Sequence cannot contain non-ATGC bases')
    length = len(dna)
    a_count = dna.count('A')
    t_count = dna.count('T')
    at_content = (a_count + t_count) / length
    return at_content

sequences = ['ACGTACGTGAC', 'ACTGCTNAACT', 'ATGGCGCTAGC']
for seq in sequences:
    try:
        print('AT content for ' + seq + ' is ' + str(get_at_content(seq)))
    except AmbiguousBaseError:
        print('skipping invalid sequence '+ seq)
```

custom_error.py

---

1 If that sentence doesn't make sense, take a look at the chapter on object oriented programming for an explanation of inheritance.
2 In Python, pass is just a place holder bit of code that means "do nothing".

Now any exceptions raised by `get_at_content()` will not get mixed up with exceptions raised in other parts of the code. As a nice side benefit, the code is now clearer, as the name of the error class is a concise description of what it means.

Custom exception types are just examples of classes, so we can treat them just like any other custom class. For example, we can add members and methods to them, although that's not usually helpful. More interestingly, we can also build use inheritance to place them in class hierarchies, which can sometimes be useful when building complex class systems[1].

Recap

Whenever we write code that relies on some data or resources being supplied by an external source, we have to consider ways in which those data or resources might cause a problem for our code. Two common examples are when writing code that relies on user input (or on the contents of external files), and when writing library-type code that might be used by another programmer. Python's exception system offers an elegant way both to respond to problems that occur in built in functions and methods, and to report problems that occur in our own code.

We started the chapter by looking at how exception handlers allow us to catch and deal with exceptions in a very flexible way – we can choose exactly what kinds of exceptions we wish to handle and can write arbitrary code to do so, and can choose at which level of the code exceptions should be handled. We can even interrogate exceptions to get extra information about the problem that occurred.

Raising exceptions, on the other hand, allows us to signal that something has gone wrong in our code, resulting in (hopefully) helpful error

---

[1] See the solution to the second exercise in this chapter for a fairly minimal example.

messages, and giving the calling code a chance to correct it. Python has a range of built in exception types to represent common problems, but if we need something more specific then we can easily create our own.

Using exceptions – rather than lengthy `if`/`else` conditions and `print()` statements – to handle errors results in better code. Code that uses exceptions tends to be more robust, since it allows us to deal with problems when they actually arise, rather than trying to pre-emptively catch them. It also tends to be more readable, since error-handling code is clearly demarcated and the syntax of the exception handling system makes it clear which type of errors are being handled.

Some readers might find the examples presented in this chapter unconvincing. This is likely a reflection of the fact that exception handling is most valuable in large projects and library code, neither of which lend themselves to concise examples (or to exercises in programming books). As your programming projects become larger and more complicated, you'll find that the encapsulation offered by exceptions far outweighs the extra mental overhead of thinking about them.

Chapter 7: Exception handling

Exercises

Responding to exceptions

A Python programmer has written a piece of code that reads a DNA sequence from a file and splits it up into a set number of equal-sized pieces (ignoring any incomplete pieces at the end of the sequence). It asks the user to enter the name of the file and the number of pieces, calculates the length of each piece (by dividing the total length by the number of pieces), then uses a `range()` to print out each piece:

```
# ask the user for the filename, open it and read the DNA sequence
input_file = raw_input('enter filename:\n')
f = open(input_file)
dna = f.read().rstrip("\n")

# ask the user for the number of pieces and calculate the piece length
pieces = int(raw_input('enter number of pieces:\n'))
piece_length = len(dna) / pieces
print('piece length is ' + str(piece_length))

# print out each piece of DNA in turn
for start in range(0, len(dna)-piece_length+1, piece_length):
    print(dna[start:start+piece_length])
```

original.py

The code works well enough, but after playing around with it for a while, the programmer realizes that it's quite easy to make it crash by, for example, giving it the name of a non-existent file, or entering zero when asked for the number of pieces – or indeed, entering something that isn't a number at all when asked for the number of pieces.

The programmer decides to make the code more robust by checking for these three errors at each step of the program before proceeding to the next step. That way, if it looks like the user has entered an invalid file name, or an incorrect number, the program can exit gracefully with a useful error message. The programmer decides to use the `os` module to check for a file at the given path, the string `isdigit` method to check that the user has entered an integer, a normal `if` condition to check that the integer is greater than zero, and the `sys.exit` method to quit the program if any of these things are wrong. Here's the code that they come up with:

```
import os
import sys

# check for valid filename
input_file = raw_input('enter filename:\n')
if not os.path.isfile(input_file):
    sys.exit('not a valid filename')
f = open(input_file)
dna = f.read().rstrip("\n")

# check for valid number
pieces = raw_input('enter number of pieces:\n')
if not pieces.isdigit():
    sys.exit('not a valid number')

# check that number is not zero or negative
pieces = int(pieces)
if pieces < 0:
    sys.exit('number of pieces must be greater than zero')

# do the processing
piece_length = len(dna) / pieces
print('piece length is ' + str(piece_length))
for start in range(0, len(dna)-piece_length+1, piece_length):
    print(dna[start:start+piece_length])
```

`original_with_if.py`

Unfortunately, the programmer didn't know that using exception handlers to cope with these errors would be much better and result in more readable code. Rewrite this code to use error handlers instead of `if` statements.

Chapter 7: Exception handling

Exceptions for the SequenceRecord classes

Take a look back at the classes that we designed for working with DNA and protein sequences in the chapter on object oriented programming. Here's a reminder of the class code (with method bodies left out for readability):

```
class SequenceRecord(object):

    def __init__(self, sequence, gene_name, species_name):
        self.sequence = sequence
        self.gene_name = gene_name
        self.species_name = species_name

    def get_fasta(self):
        ...

class ProteinRecord(SequenceRecord):

    def get_hydrophobic(self):
        ...

class DNARecord(SequenceRecord):

    def complement(self):
        ...

    def get_AT(self):
        ...
```

As implemented above, the `SequenceRecord` constructor doesn't have any kind of error checking. There is nothing to prevent us from creating a `DNARecord` object with all kinds of invalid properties:

```
# invalid bases in the sequence
d = DNARecord('ATGYCNNCR', 'COX1', 'Homo sapiens')

# an empty string for the gene name
d = DNARecord('ATGCGGTGA', '', 'Homo sapiens')

# an incorrectly-formatted species name
d = DNARecord('ATGCGGTGA', 'COX1', 'homosapiens')
```

We can even do completely inappropriate things like create a `DNARecord` where the properties are not even strings:

```
d = DNARecord(3.1415, 42, -1)
```

Modify the class definitions to raise exceptions if we try to create objects with invalid properties.

Chapter 7: Exception handling

Solutions

Responding to exceptions

The first step in rewriting the code is to go back to the original code and figure out exactly what kind of errors we are dealing with. We know from the examples earlier in the chapter that we'll get an `IOError` if we try to open a file that isn't there, and that we'll get a `ValueError` if we try to turn an inappropriate string into an integer using the `int()` function. We can easily find out what happens when we ask for the DNA to be split into zero pieces by running the first version of the code and giving the relevant input:

```
enter filename:
test.dna
enter number of pieces:
0
Traceback (most recent call last):
  File "adding.py", line 8, in <module>
    piece_length = len(dna) / pieces
ZeroDivisionError: integer division or modulo by zero
```

It turns out that we get a `ZeroDivisionError` when we try to calculate the piece length by dividing the DNA sequence length by the number of pieces. Armed with this information, it's just a question of wrapping the brittle code inside a `try` block, adding the appropriate `except` blocks, and adding an `else` block to print the results if everything is OK:

```
try:
    # ask the user for the filename, open it and read the DNA sequence
    input_file = raw_input('enter filename:\n')
    f = open(input_file)
    dna = f.read().rstrip("\n")

    # ask the user for the number of pieces and calculate the piece length
    pieces = int(raw_input('enter number of pieces:\n'))
    piece_length = len(dna) / pieces
    print('piece length is ' + str(piece_length))
except IOError:
    print("Couldn't open the file")
except ValueError:
    print("Not a valid number")
except ZeroDivisionError:
    print("Number of pieces can't be zero")
else:
    # print out each piece of DNA in turn
    for start in range(0, len(dna)-piece_length+1, piece_length):
        print(dna[start:start+piece_length])
```

When comparing the code above with the solution offered in the exercise description there are two things to notice. Firstly although it's not any shorter, it's much easier to read because the code for dealing with input errors is all collected in one place (the group of **except** blocks) rather than being mixed up with the rest of the code.

Secondly, it is able to deal with a wider range of potential problems. For instance, consider the case where the specified input file exists, but its permissions are set such that it isn't readable by the program. Testing if the file exists using **os.path.exists**, as was done in the previous solution, will return **True**, but the program will still produce an error when trying to open it. However, in our approach above, the **IOError** that is raised when trying to open the file will still be caught and dealt with. In light of this fact, we can probably make our error message in the event of an **IOError** more helpful, by printing out the details alongside our own error message:

Chapter 7: Exception handling

```
...
except IOError as ex:
    print("Couldn't open the file: " + ex.strerror)
...
```

We can also make the `ValueError` message more helpful by printing out its details – recall that these are stored in a list called `args` and that the first element is the message we want:

```
...
except ValueError as ex:
    print("Not a valid number: " + ex.args[0])
...
```

Here's the whole thing put together:

```
try:
    # ask the user for the filename, open it and read the DNA sequence
    input_file = raw_input('enter filename:\n')
    f = open(input_file)
    dna = f.read().rstrip("\n")

    # ask the user for the number of pieces and calculate the piece length
    pieces = int(raw_input('enter number of pieces:\n'))
    piece_length = len(dna) / pieces
    print('piece length is ' + str(piece_length))
except IOError as ex:
    print("Couldn't open the file: " + ex.strerror)
except ValueError as ex:
    print("Not a valid number: " + ex.args[0])
except ZeroDivisionError as ex:
    print("Number of pieces can't be zero")
else:
    # print out each piece of DNA in turn
    for start in range(0, len(dna)-piece_length+1, piece_length):
        print(dna[start:start+piece_length])
```

responding.py

Exceptions for the SequenceRecord classes

Tackling this problem is going to involve a combination of techniques from this chapter and the one on object oriented programming, so make sure you've read both before proceeding.

We know that, when writing classes, it's the constructor that's responsible for creating a new object based on the arguments that are passed to it, so that seems like a logical place to put our validation code. Let's start with a simple bit of validation: we don't want to allow empty strings as gene names, so we'll just check the length of the gene name and raise an error if it's equal to zero. We want this behaviour to apply to both `DNARecord` and `ProteinRecord` objects, so we'll add it to the constructor of the base class `SequenceRecord`[1]:

```
class SequenceRecord(object):

    def __init__(self, sequence, gene_name, species_name):
        if len(gene_name) == 0:
            raise ValueError('gene name cannot be empty')
        self.sequence = sequence
        self.gene_name = gene_name
        self.species_name = species_name

    def get_fasta(self):
        ...
```

This will cause a `ValueError` to be raised (and an error message printed, if it's not caught) if we try to do something like this:

```
d = DNARecord('ATGCGGTGA', '', 'Homo sapiens')
```

Note that we could have created a custom error type – perhaps called `EmptyGeneNameError` – to raise here. The choice of whether to use a built in Python exception or a custom one generally boils down to: are

---
1   Take a look at the section on inheritance in the chapter on object oriented programming for a reminder about base and derived classes.

Chapter 7: Exception handling

you frequently going to want to write exception handlers **just** to handle this particular situation? To a large extent, this depends on how you anticipate the code being used.

This validation check has an interesting side-effect; it also raises an error if we try to pass in a number as a gene name:

```
d = DNARecord('ATGCGGTGA', 42, 'Homo sapiens')
```
```
TypeError: object of type 'int' has no len()
```

but notice that the exception is raised by the call to `len()` (since integers don't have a length) and hence is a `TypeError` rather than a `ValueError`. There are a couple of different approaches we can take to the possibility of a non-string gene name. We might want to be flexible, and allow a `SequenceRecord` object to be created with any type of object as a gene name, in which case we need to convert the gene_name variable to a string before checking its length:

```
class SequenceRecord(object):

    def __init__(self, sequence, gene_name, species_name):
        if len(str(gene_name)) == 0:
            raise ValueError('gene name cannot be empty')
        self.sequence = sequence
        self.gene_name = gene_name
        self.species_name = species_name

    def get_fasta(self):
        ...
```

If we take this approach, then we can create a `SequenceRecord` with 42 as the gene name argument, which will get converted to the string "42" when the length of the gene name is checked. In fact we can pass in **any** type of data as the gene name argument, since all Python objects can be represented as strings – which may not be what we want.

Alternatively, we can decide to be very strict and **only** accept strings as gene name arguments. We can enforce this by adding another validation check which raises a `TypeError` if the gene name isn't a string:

```
class SequenceRecord(object):

    def __init__(self, sequence, gene_name, species_name):
        if not isinstance(gene_name, str):
            raise TypeError('gene name must be a string')
        if len(gene_name) == 0:
            raise ValueError('gene name cannot be empty')
        self.sequence = sequence
        self.gene_name = gene_name
        self.species_name = species_name

    def get_fasta(self):
        ...
```

The choice of whether to be strict or flexible about argument types is a complex one and depends largely on how we anticipate the code being used. We must be careful, however, when programming in Python not to end up abusing exceptions to recreate the type systems of statically-typed languages like Java.

On to the next problem – checking that the species name passed to the constructor is properly-formatted. Let's first specify what we mean by properly-formatted: we want to check that the species name is in exactly two parts separated by a single space, and that everything is in lower case except for the first character, which must be in upper case. We can write a regular expression to match this pattern:

```
r"[A-Z][a-z]+ [a-z]+"
```

Chapter 7: Exception handling

which we'll use in the `re.match()` function rather than the more usual `re.search` because we want to match the entire string rather than just a part of it:

```
import re
class SequenceRecord(object):

    def __init__(self, sequence, gene_name, species_name):
        gene_name = str(gene_name)
        if not isinstance(gene_name, str):
            raise TypeError('gene name must be a string')
        if len(gene_name) == 0:
            raise ValueError('gene name cannot be empty')

        # check for valid species name
        if not re.match(r"[A-Z][a-z]+ [a-z]+", species_name):
            raise ValueError('species name incorrectly formatted')
        self.sequence = sequence
        self.gene_name = gene_name
        self.species_name = species_name

    def get_fasta(self):
        ...
```

The appropriate exception to raise here is a `ValueError`, since if the regular expression match executes successfully (even if the pattern itself fails to match) then we know that the argument must have been a string. Just like before, we can takes things a step further if we want and check the type of the argument as well.

We've saved the trickiest part of the exercise for last: how to prevent `SequenceRecord` objects being created with invalid characters. The reason that this part is difficult is that, unlike the previous checks, our criteria here are different for `DNARecord` objects (where we want to only allow nucleic acid codes) and `ProteinRecord` objects (where we want to only allow amino acid residue codes). The checks themselves are fairly straightforward:

```
if re.search(r'[^ATGC]', some_dna_sequence):
        # raise an exception

if re.search(r'[^FLSYCWPHQRIMTNKVADEG]', some_protein_sequence):
        # raise an exception
```

but the question is where to put them. There are two good options[1]: either we could override the base class constructor in each of the derived classes, or we could add a validation method to the derived classes which can be called by the superclass constructor. The first approach is probably the most object oriented: it follows the principal of allowing derived classes to inherit general functionality from the base class while adding functionality that is specific to themselves. Take a look at the chapter on object oriented programming, specifically the section on overriding methods in the base class, for an example of this type of validation.

Because we've already seen an example of the first approach in a previous chapter, we'll try the second one here so that we have seen an example of both. To do this we simply add a sequence validation method to each of the derived classes (`DNARecord` and `ProteinRecord`) and call it in the constructor of the parent class (`SequenceRecord`) as the last step before actually assigning the arguments. The magic of inheritance ensures that when the sequence validation method is called in the constructor, the appropriate subclass method is executed depending on whether we are creating a `DNARecord` or a `ProteinRecord`.

Because we're intending the sequence validation method to only be called in the base class constructor, we can take advantage of the Python formatting convention that methods beginning with an underscore are for internal use only. This isn't enforced by the language in any way, but it's a useful hint to anyone looking at the source code that they shouldn't call the sequence validation method for any other reason. Here's the code:

---

1 And more than a few bad ones, which we won't discuss here!

Chapter 7: Exception handling

```
import re
class SequenceRecord(object):

    def __init__(self, sequence, gene_name, species_name):
        gene_name = str(gene_name)
        if not isinstance(gene_name, str):
            raise TypeError('gene name must be a string')
        if len(gene_name) == 0:
            raise ValueError('gene name cannot be empty')
        if not re.match(r"[A-Z][a-z]+ [a-z]+", species_name):
            raise ValueError('species name incorrectly formatted')

        # validate the sequence before we assign it
        self._validate_sequence(sequence)
        self.sequence = sequence
        self.gene_name = gene_name
        self.species_name = species_name

    ...

class ProteinRecord(SequenceRecord):

    def _validate_sequence(self, sequence):
        if re.search(r'[^FLSYCWPHQRIMTNKVADEG]', sequence):
            raise ValueError("invalid amino acid code in sequence")

    ...

class DNARecord(SequenceRecord):

    def _validate_sequence(self, sequence):
        if re.search(r'[^ATGC]', sequence):
            raise ValueError("invalid base in sequence")

    ...
```

Because these type types of error fall into a natural hierarchy – they are both examples of invalid sequences – let's create a few custom exception classes to represent them. We'll write a base class, **InvalidCharacterError**, which inherits from the **Exception** class, then add two derived classes to represent errors in DNA and protein sequences which will inherit from the base class. Here are the class definitions for the exceptions – we don't need them to do anything that isn't implemented by the `Exception` class, so the class definition body can just be `pass` in each case:

```
class InvalidCharacterError(Exception):
    pass

class InvalidBaseError(InvalidCharacterError):
    pass

class InvalidAminoAcidError(InvalidCharacterError):
    pass
```

sequence_record.py

And here are the modifications that we have to make to the validation methods:

```
class ProteinRecord(SequenceRecord):

    def validate_sequence(self, sequence):
      if re.search(r'[^FLSYCWPHQRIMTNKVADEG]', sequence):
          raise InvalidAminoAcidError("invalid amino acid code in sequence")

    ...


class DNARecord(SequenceRecord):

    def validate_sequence(self, sequence):
      if re.search(r'[^ATGC]', sequence):
          raise InvalidBaseError("invalid base in sequence")
    ...
```

sequence_record.py

Using a hierarchy of custom exceptions in this way allows us to write an exception handler that can cope with any type of error caused by an invalid character:

Chapter 7: Exception handling

```
except InvalidCharacterError:
    # deal with the invalid sequence
```

as well as exception handlers that only catch particular types (i.e. DNA or protein) of error.

Afterword

This is the end of *Advanced Python for biologists*; I hope you have enjoyed the book, and found it useful. Remember that if you have any comments on the book – good or bad – I'd love to hear them; drop me an email at

    martin@pythonforbiologists.com

If you think that you might end up using the techniques you've learned in this book to build larger Python programs, then take a look at the companion book *Effective Python development for Biologists*, which contains detailed discussions of topics that you're likely to run into – things like how to test your code, and how to build a user interface.

If you've found the book useful, please also consider leaving a Amazon **review**. Reviews will help other people to find the book, and hopefully make learning Python a bit easier for everyone.

Index

A
alleles 92
AmbiguousBaseError 201
anonymous expression 115
anonymous values 42
args 187
AT content 78, 118, 122, 154
AttributeError 73
autovivification 60

B
base class 69, 80
BLAST 138
bugs 180

C
call stack 23
catching exceptions 182
child to parent 16
children 26
clades 54
class 65, 69
comma-separated fields 105
comments 142
complex sorts 128
composition 64
comprehensions 158
constructor 74, 86
context managers 192

D
defining a class 68
derived class 80
dict comprehension 61

dict comprehensions *50*
dictionary comprehensions *163*
dicts of lists *48*
dicts of sets *45*
dicts of tuples *47*
difference *40*
dinucleotides *14*
distance matrices *57*
duplicate elements *38*

E
else *188*
encapsulation *65*
except *182, 184*
exception bubbling *194*
exceptions *181*
exhaustible expressions *162*
extend() *110*

F
FASTA format *76, 139*
filter *122, 146*
finally *189*
fitness *92*
function factory *134*
functional programming *109*

G
generation *105*
generator expressions *161*
generators *169*

H
heterogeneous data *37*
higher-order functions *113, 131*
homogeneous data *38*

I

immutable	37
inheritance	64, 76
instance	65
instance variables	68
intersection	40, 57
InvalidAminoAcidError	217
InvalidBaseError	217
InvalidCharacterError	216
IOError	183
isdigit	205
isinstance()	53
issubset method	46
iter	166
iterable objects	158
iterable types	166
iterator interface	166
itertools	178

K

key functions	125
kmer counting	49
kmers	9, 132
kmers()	170

L

lambda expression	134
Last Common Ancestor	30, 55, 130
lazy evaluation	122
list comprehension	46
list comprehensions	159
lists of dicts	42
lists of lists	40
lists of tuples	42

M

map	117

metadata *67*
methods *68*
mismatches *142*
monopyly *57*
multiple sequence alignment *41*
mutability *109*

N
nested comprehensions *62, 162*
nested lists *51*
Newick format *51*
next *167*
node *28*

O
object *65*
object-oriented programming *64*
os.path.exists *209*
overriding *85*

P
pairwise comparison *47*
pairwise comparisons *163*
parent to child *16*
parents *19*
partial function application *136*
phylogenetic trees *51*
poly-A tail *126, 139*
polymorphism *64, 89*
pop() ❷ *26*
population *92*
primers *172*
pure functions *113*

R
raise *197*
raising exceptions *197*
random *96*

re.match 214
Recursion 9
reduce 129
restriction enzymes 134

S

self 69
set comprehensions 165
Sets 38
side effects 110
simulation 92
sliding window 132
sorted 124
stable sort 128
stack 27
state 109
StopIteration 167
strerror 186
sub 152
subclass 80
subsets 46
subtrees 53
sum 110
superclass 80
syntax errors 180

T

taxonomy 16
transformation function 118
translation 84
tree 16
trees 51
trinucletoides 14
try 182
Tuples 36
two-dimensional list 40
TypeError 212

U
union 40, 57
unpacking tuples 45

V
ValueError 183

Y
yield 169

Z
ZeroDivisionError 208

_
__init__() 74
__iter__ 166